Classroom Management

24 Strategies Every Teacher Needs to Know

DAVID R. ADAMSON

New York • Toronto • London • Auckland • Sydney **Teaching** *Resources*
Mexico City • New Delhi • Hong Kong • Buenos Aires

I want to acknowledge the major contributions of two administrators, Annette Brinkman and Tim Frost, whose efforts to assist teachers having trouble managing student behavior are saving dozens of careers every year. Thanks are certainly due to my many teaching friends who have been so generous with their time and suggestions. I also want to thank my wife, Nyla, herself a 38-year veteran of elementary and junior high classrooms, for her expert advice and her patience through this project.

Editor: Mela Ottaiano
Cover design and photographs: Maria Lilja
Interior design and illustrations: Melinda Belter
ISBN-13: 978-0-545-19569-0
ISBN-10: 0-545-19569-1

Contents

Introduction 5

CHAPTER 1

What It Takes to Control Your Class: 9
KEY ELEMENTS TO CONSIDER

Preventative Management Practices 11

Positive Relationships 11

Instruction 13

Interventions 13

Professionalism 14

CHAPTER 2

Preventative Management Practices: 15
THE FUNDAMENTALS FOR BRINGING ORDER TO YOUR CLASS

STRATEGY 1 • Social Cues 15

STRATEGY 2 • Attention Signal 21

STRATEGY 3 • Use Self-Starters 25

STRATEGY 4 • Proximity Control 28

STRATEGY 5 • Time Limits 31

STRATEGY 6 • Seating Arrangements 36

STRATEGY 7 • Manage Your Transitions 40

STRATEGY 8 • Teach Classroom Rules and Procedures 45

CHAPTER 3

Positive Relationships: 49
CARE, TRUST, AND RESPECT

STRATEGY 9 • Show That You Care 51

STRATEGY 10 • Build Trust 56

STRATEGY 11 • Show Respect 60

CHAPTER 4

Instruction: 65
HARNESS THE POWER OF AN INTERESTING LESSON

    STRATEGY 12 • Get Your Students Participating 66

    STRATEGY 13 • Keep Your Pacing Crisp and Your Students Active 71

    STRATEGY 14 • Plan Lessons With Crafty Care 77

CHAPTER 5

Interventions: 87
WHEN THEY MISBEHAVE, *DO* SOMETHING

    STRATEGY 15 • The Clipboard Technique 88

    STRATEGY 16 • Target Behavior.. 92

    STRATEGY 17 • "In the Moment" Interventions 96

    STRATEGY 18 • Directed Response Interventions 98

    STRATEGY 19 • Private Conference Interventions 103

CHAPTER 6

Professionalism: 115
KEEPING IT ALL TOGETHER

    STRATEGY 20 • Adopt a Formal Management Structure 116

    STRATEGY 21 • Teach and Use Routines 123

    STRATEGY 22 • Keep Up 127

    STRATEGY 23 • Keep Your Cool 131

    STRATEGY 24 • Getting Started . . . Again!................................... 134

CHAPTER 7

Teaching Is a Team Sport: 137
GETTING HELP WHEN HELP IS NEEDED

    Where to Turn 137

References 139

Appendix 141

Introduction

• • •

Over the past three years I have been working almost exclusively with new teachers. Not just any new teachers but those who are struggling with classroom behavior. Despite having a genuine concern for their students and the highest of motives, they typically lack a few key strategies for managing the behavior of their students. The climate in their classrooms can range from daily tension to absolute bedlam. But when these teachers take the time to learn effective strategies and grow the courage to use them consistently, classrooms come to order. Their new profession becomes a source of joy. The purpose of this book is to share a short collection of very powerful strategies and methods that will help any teacher prevent problems, intervene when problems arise, and maintain a controlled classroom through the entire school year.

The teaching profession holds excitement, challenge, variety, meaningful impact, and just plain fun. It is said that teaching is the mother of all professions, for it is a teacher who prepares the next generation to enter each of the other professions. However, it is also a tough profession. You are responsible not only for creating an environment of learning but also for the safety of students who are legally compelled to remain in the environment you create. You are the manager of both learning *and* security while these young people are in your charge.

Not Just for Teachers

▲ Many school districts are now designating "mentor teachers" who help other teachers who are having concerns about student behavior. Mentors are there to give pointers and share their experience. If you are a mentor, you will find easily referenced descriptions of the strategies you are most likely to recommend. Recommending a specific strategy or two makes it much more likely that the receiving teacher will benefit from the help. It is so much more personal than simply handing someone another book with a casual, "Here, just read this."

▲ If you are a principal or assistant principal who evaluates teachers, you will also find this book valuable. Like the role of the mentor, the more prescriptive and specific a school administration can be, the greater the likelihood that student behavior will improve and the teacher will become more successful.

Here, then, is your challenge: to manage your many responsibilities and make a difference in the lives of children. You cannot teach if student behavior issues are dominating your time. You cannot enjoy this exciting profession if conflict and confrontation are constantly sapping your energy.

For most teachers, the toughest part of teaching is managing student behavior. As you have no doubt experienced, your students must be under control before they can learn. Your goal is to make managing classroom behavior so routine that you can focus your energy on teaching.

If student behavior in your classroom has been getting in the way of your ability to teach and the students' ability to learn, it is time to try something different. Dr. Ellen Williams (1996) gives all teachers the reassurance that getting control of your class is possible. Like anything else, she explains, it will take time and preparation up front. But your students need you *this* year, so you need to take immediate steps to get your classroom under control *now*.

This guide is intended to shorten your learning curve. The 24 classroom management strategies, each with its own easily referenced, stand-alone description, can save you hours of time—not to mention many sleepless nights. *It's precisely because they are not new that they are so effective.* These strategies have been used and adapted by successful teachers. They are intended for 90–95% of your students, the mainstream of your class. They have been compiled in this concise format to get you quickly to exactly the strategies you need to keep your class under control.

While every teacher should know these strategies, differences in classrooms will dictate different priorities. Peruse the strategies and focus first on your most pressing areas of concern. Start with the fundamentals you will find in Chapter 2. Then pick up this book again and again to develop and refine the others. Most classroom management issues will be resolved with the consistent use of these first eight strategies. One or more of these strategies may be helpful, but apply the one that feels the most natural for you to be more effective.

REFLECTION QUESTION

**What specific strategy could I use with this particular
class in this particular situation to address this
specific behavior problem?**

Nothing in this book is intended to replace the personal, face-to-face conversations with mentors or administrators. The relationships developed in these conversations are essential and invaluable. This collection of strategies is intended to enhance your conversation. Above all, remember that while this is a tough profession, it is far more rewarding when managing student behavior does not dominate your time and attention.

CHAPTER 1

What It Takes to Control Your Class:

KEY ELEMENTS TO CONSIDER

• • •

It takes more than luck to control your class.

Sure, it would be nice if you could hand-select your students. It would be great if all of your students came from homes that completely supported their teachers. It would be wonderful if all teachers had a charismatic personality that naturally inspired their students to follow the rules. But that is not reality.

What we do know is that there are a few, very specific strategies that teachers can use to manage their classroom. Learning these strategies and applying them consistently will improve student behavior in the classroom as well as student achievement. In his meta-analysis of more than 100 classroom management studies, Marzano (2003) finds that, on average, students in classes where effective behavior management strategies are used have engagement rates that are 23 percentile points higher and achievement scores that are 20 percentile points higher than those of students in classes where these strategies are not used. He concludes that,

"Good classroom managers are teachers who understand and use specific techniques. Awareness and training in these techniques can change teacher behavior, which in turn changes student behavior and ultimately affects student achievement positively. Again, research evidence supports this assertion."

(Robert Marzano, 2003)

Structuring Your Practice

The strategies described in this book are derived from some basic assumptions about behavior:

• Prevention is more effective than intervention.

• A positive relationship is your most powerful management tool.

• There is no substitute for good instruction.

• Effective interventions are those that change behavior while preserving the dignity of both students and teachers.

• Professionalism is a key to establishing yourself as an effective classroom manager.

Preventative Management Practices

The first and most important key to managing classroom behavior is to prevent misbehavior from occurring in the first place. It's like preventive maintenance for a car or preventive medicine for our own health. The best way to maintain the health of your car, your body, or your classroom is to address potential problems before they happen.

The way you conduct your class and the management practices you use will actually determine the number of classroom management problems you will face. If you have concerns about student behavior, you must be willing to change *your* routines in order to influence *their* behavior. The first eight management strategies, described in Chapter 2, are designed to prevent student misbehavior in class.

Positive Relationships

The most powerful motivator for students to improve their behavior is the desire to maintain a positive relationship with their teacher. Once a positive relationship has been established, the reason they will follow the class rules shifts from fear of punishment to the desire to please. They will change their behavior because they do not want to damage their relationship with you. That is the reason that developing and maintaining a positive relationship with your students early in the year pays such big dividends throughout the year.

It is crucial to remember that we are working with young human beings. An environment of intimidation, domination, and ridicule will do more to damage classroom behavior than help. On the flip side, an environment of anarchy without enforced expectations creates fear, uncertainty, and doubt. Teaching in either environment is not fun. It drains the teacher's energy, and over time it is actually counterproductive. In stark contrast, an environment of respect and personal dignity grows a climate of self-discipline.

The 24 Strategies

1. Social Cues
2. Attention Signal
3. Use Self-Starters
4. Proximity Control
5. Time Limits
6. Seating Arrangements
7. Manage Your Transitions
8. Teach Classroom Rules and Procedures
9. Show That You Care
10. Build Trust
11. Show Respect
12. Get Your Students Participating
13. Keep Your Pacing Crisp and Your Students Active
14. Plan Lessons With Crafty Care
15. The Clipboard Technique
16. Target Behavior
17. "In the Moment" Interventions
18. Directed Response Interventions
19. Private Conference Interventions
20. Adopt a Formal Management Structure
21. Teach and Use Routines
22. Keep Up
23. Keep Your Cool
24. Getting Started . . . Again!

Students know that their misbehavior causes stress and pain for teachers. That's OK with them if they see their teacher as an automated bureaucrat or a stern authoritarian. But when they care about their teacher and know that their teacher cares about them, things are very different. It is tough to jeopardize a relationship with someone who you believe genuinely cares about you. Misbehaving risks damaging a valuable relationship. Relationships are built with students in the same way that they are built with family and friends. We get back what we give. Strategies 9–11, described in Chapter 3, show how to grow positive relationships with young people.

Instruction

We should never underestimate the power that a well-designed lesson has over student behavior. A good lesson is one that is well prepared, moves along at a crisp pace, and differentiates for students with different needs. It has a clear answer to the question, "Besides sit and listen, what will the students *do*?" When students do not have a clear task, they will most certainly find something else to do. When a lesson is dull, seems to drag, and feels overly repetitive, students will find their own ways to make the time they spend in class interesting.

In Chapter 4, Strategies 12–14, along with some descriptions of specific teaching methods, show how to keep students productively involved in the content of the curriculum. Students who are engaged in learning are so much less likely to create behavior problems for their teachers.

Interventions

All students occasionally misbehave—it is in their very nature. It happens in the best of classes. While our organizational practices, positive relationships, and instructional design can reduce the amount of misbehavior, they will never eliminate it completely. The lesson here is that the way you respond to misbehavior today will affect the behavior of your entire class tomorrow.

Question: How much corrective action should you be using?

Answer: The minimum amount needed to do the job.

The point of correcting misbehavior is to allow teaching and learning to continue smoothly and safely. If we accomplish that with minimal effort and with the student's dignity intact, we have succeeded.

Certainly when misbehavior occurs, we need to intervene. What's critical is that we select an intervention that minimizes the time taken away from instruction. The other students must be able to continue learning while you pause briefly to deal with the problem. The intervention must be effective enough to change the behavior and efficient enough to create only a blip in the flow of your lesson. It becomes elegant when it can achieve all of these *and* enhance the relationship between you and the student.

Strategies 15–19 in Chapter 5 are all very powerful. Most are subtle and some even benevolent. Some can change behavior without a word; others can actually make the teacher-student relationship stronger. You will find a menu of interventions from which you can choose, using your professional judgment and growing experience.

Professionalism

It may sound simplistic, but too frequently I find it necessary to remind new teachers that they need to know what is going on in their classroom. When a teacher is not watching, anything is fair game. The teacher is the single most significant factor that determines classroom behavior. Chapter 6 describes Strategies 20–24, which will help you to stay in touch with what is happening in your classroom. It provides a description of formal management structures to clearly define for students your expectations and how you will respond to their behavior. It outlines routines that give students predictability and confidence in the classroom. The chapter also provides suggestions for keeping your professional cool when your authority is challenged. Finally, you will find some considerations in managing the change process if you want to implement new classroom procedures after the school year is already well under way.

CHAPTER 2

Preventative Management Practices:

THE FUNDAMENTALS FOR BRINGING ORDER TO YOUR CLASS

● ● ●

So many roots of student behavior problems can be directly traced to problems in our procedures and practices. In reviewing ten studies of classroom management describing rules and procedures, Robert Marzano (2003) found that the average number of disruptions was 28 percentile points lower in classrooms where rules and procedures were effectively implemented when compared to classrooms where they were not. These organizational structures and management practices are critical tools for prevention. This chapter describes eight powerful organizational practices and procedures that can make a real difference in the behavior of your class.

STRATEGY 1 ▶ Social Cues

If you take away only one skill from this book, choose this one. This is the single most powerful skill any teacher can possess. It is inexpensive, powerful, convenient, easy to use, and highly portable. With one well-placed application it can correct, clarify, reinforce, and signal the rest of the class.

Essential Components of a Social Cue

Briefly state an observable desired behavior that you want to see in class. It should be

- attributed to a specific student who is modeling that behavior

- articulated loud enough for the entire class or group to hear

- targeted to areas of teacher concern

- providing an affirming example of **successful behavior**

A social cue is a simple statement that a teacher makes to the class. An effective cue clearly restates an observable behavior that you are expecting of the class and highlights a specific student who is demonstrating the desired behavior. This provides students the cue they need to correct their own behavior and indicates that this desired behavior helps you. It signals to the class that you are, indeed, monitoring their behavior and that you expect compliance with your expectations.

Annette Brinkman (2009) tells us that social cues are a secondary source, not a primary source, of behavior management. They are used to assist with making transitions, bringing the class to order, maintaining desired behavior, and calling for attention. Their use makes the other strategies work better.

Student misbehavior is *your* cue to use social cues. For example, two students begin talking to each other. This is your signal to use a social cue, pointing out by name that two or three others sitting close to these students are complying with your expectations. You do not need to single out the students who are talking. The message was sent, and the students who are talking will almost always respond.

You will need to create your own social cues based on the circumstances at the moment. Ellen Williams (1996) recommends first visualizing what you want the students to be doing. "What should their behavior sound like or look like?" The answers to this question are your social cues. The examples listed below are useful models to help you get started.

A caveat: social cues should not be overused. Two or three should be sufficient for each directive or transition. Neither should they ever be used with sarcasm, because you risk losing one of your most valuable tools. Avoid formulaic statements; they sound insincere ("I like the way Bob is sitting quietly. I like the way Josh is sitting quietly. I like the way Carmen is sitting quietly."). When used well, a few well-placed social cues can have an amazing impact on the behavior of a class of students. Seeing how they can help you establish the positive environment you would like to see in your classroom is extremely satisfying.

Examples of Social Cues for Grades 3–5:

▶ "I noticed Emily has opened her book and is already beginning to work on her assignment. Thank you, Emily."

1. (statement of desired behavior)	"opened her book" and "beginning to work"
2. (attributed to a specific student)	Emily
3. (articulated loud enough for others to hear)	level of voice
4. (targeted to area of teacher concern)	students dawdling in starting their work
5. (affirming example of desired behavior)	"I noticed" and "thank you"

▶ "Jacob and Chris have put their pencils down, their eyes are on me, and they are sitting up, straight, ready to go."

▶ "I have noticed that the green group is using six-inch [or *appropriate*, for older grades] voices, and every single person in that group is helping with the . . ."

▶ "I want everyone to look at Madison and Hannah. They are standing quietly in line, facing forward with their arms folded. I can certainly tell that they are ready to go."

▶ "I see that Brandon is walking quietly to his seat. Thank you, Brandon. And Ashley is walking quietly without touching anyone along the way. Thank you Ashley."

▶ "Wow! I really liked the quiet way that you came into the room this morning. You hung up your backpacks, quickly took your seats, and quietly started on your bell work. That is so helpful to me and I really appreciate it. When you come back from recess, I will be standing right here to see if you can do it that well once again."

▶ "When I tell you to go, I will be watching to see how quietly and quickly you can put away your books, get up from your desk, and quietly take your place on the rug. Ready . . . go. Good. I see Jessica walking quietly . . . Matthew is sitting quietly with his eyes on me . . . Nichole's desk is cleared . . . Emma is helping Miguel with his wheelchair."

▶ "Everyone at Table 2 is seated, their desks are clear, and their eyes are on me. Good job, Table 2!"

Examples of Social Cues for Grades 6 and Up:

▶ "Thanks, Joshua, for coming in quietly today."

▶ "I can see that Tim has started his work. Haley is writing. Thank you. Thanks also to Alex and Adriana for getting right to work."

▶ "Table 1 have their eyes on me. Thank you. Table 4 is looking up here. That's very helpful. And now I have everyone's attention. Thank you. That really helps me out."

▶ "Thanks, Taylor and Annette, for remembering to pick up your self-starter. Good job, Julene, you remembered today!"

▶ "I see Marco and Lauren have their computers on. Thank you. Elena and Tessa have started the assignment, thanks to them. Everyone in Row 3 is quietly at work. Super!"

IN PRACTICE

I watched a junior high math teacher trying to settle down her class before the bell rang at the end of the period. Her class, arranged in eight clusters of four desks, was chatting loudly. Very little math was taking place at all. She raised her voice over the noise and directed the class to quiet down before the bell rang. No effect. She called out the names of several students who were talking the loudest. No effect. She threatened that she would hold back students at a few tables after the bell rang if they didn't settle down. No effect. She directed a few individuals to go back to their assigned seats. A little effect.

Then she remembered our discussion about social cues. She found a table where students were sitting quietly, and in a voice loud enough for others to hear, she thanked them for sitting quietly and being ready to go when the bell rang. When she saw a boy who is a leader in the class and who happened to be reading quietly, she stated to the class that she noticed that TJ was ready to go. She saw another table that had, in the meantime, quieted down, so she simply announced that Table 6 was sitting quietly and ready to be dismissed when the bell rang. Despite her many and varied attempts to quiet her class, it was these three social cues that finally did the job.

POSITIVE COMMENTS

Social cues are intended to accomplish a very specific purpose and have a very specific design to accomplish that purpose. This does not mean that other positive comments are not useful. Besides social cues, a variety of positive comments are also important for classroom management. Teachers

Purposes of Positive Comments

▲ Social Cues: Reminders of expected behavior used as prompts for the entire class. ("Wayne has taken his seat and cleared his desk.")

▲ Recognition: Praise and public recognition for specific accomplishments intended to reinforce the individual or group. ("Good work, Table 2. You did a great job with your poster.")

▲ Climate-Building: Statements of success intended to establish and/or reinforce a positive environment. ("I am so lucky to have this class this year. You are so smart and just a delight to work with.")

▲ Coaching: Helping students to analyze their own performance and develop their own insights about what works for them. ("Nicely done. What do you think you did that helped you to get an "A" on that paper? What will you try next time?")

should be generous in their use of positive comments and they should also be intentional. As you reflect on your own practice, consider how you are using positive comments to not only control behavior but also to help students become more self-aware and build a positive climate in your classroom.

STRATEGY 2 ▶ Attention Signal

You can't teach unless you have their attention. Neither can you give directions, establish yourself to be in charge, ensure a safe environment, or manage an emergency. A successful teacher is able to quickly and efficiently get the attention of every student when needed.

REFLECTION QUESTION

Do I have everyone's attention when I begin talking to the class?

A frequent mistake of many teachers is to settle for something less than every student's attention. To begin a lesson without everyone's attention is to signal the students that their attention is optional and that the information you are about to provide is not really all that important. To allow a few students to continue to talk or play with objects is to give tacit permission to everyone else to ignore you if they so choose. Big mistake. You really want to communicate something very different. You want your class to absorb these messages from your actions:

1. "I am about to give you some very important information."

2. "Your attention to what I am about to say is important to me and is required in my class."

3. "I appreciate the prompt attention you give me when I ask for it."

4. "Failure to give me your attention will not be allowed."

Essential Components of the Attention Signal

- Get students ready.

- Move to the center of the class where you can be seen by all of the students.

- Use your audible and/or visible attention signal.

- Give brief eye contact to every student.

- Use two or three social cues to reinforce your expectations.

- Begin teaching immediately.

In order to convey these messages, you must give students a clear signal when you want their attention. This is called the "attention signal."

I have watched many new teachers gain the attention of the class, then turn their back to assemble handouts or rifle through a stack of papers to locate their lesson plan. In that brief moment they lose the attention they worked so hard to achieve. Other teachers ask for the attention of the class but then settle for only 80%. This signals that they were not really serious about getting student attention, and each subsequent attempt to gain the attention of the class gets progressively more difficult. Some new teachers try to talk with loud voices over the noise level of the class. They are surprised when I point out that the volume of student talk rises in response, followed by a rise in the teacher's volume, and again another rise in the students' volume. Student attention is finally achieved when the teacher loses his or her temper and resorts to yelling or threatening the class.

The attention signal is used when, and only when, you really have something important to say. The power of clear attention signals quickly degrades when they are overused, misused as a device to lower the noise level, or mis-timed because you were not really ready to proceed after you had gained their attention. Their power is strengthened when you explicitly teach them before using them, and when you show that obtaining the timely attention of the class really does matter to you.

Get students ready. If students are working independently or in small groups, walk around and give a few whispered warnings that you will soon be giving an attention signal. (e.g., [whispered] "In about 30 seconds I will be giving the class an attention signal. Just wanted you to be ready.")

Take your mark. Identify a routine place in your classroom where you want students to give their attention when you ask for it (typically the front center of the classroom). Move to that place every time you require the attention of the class. You can be either standing or sitting on a stool, as long as every student can clearly see you. When obtaining student attention becomes more routine, you can vary your location in the class occasionally. However, you will find that having a consistent location for using the attention signal for the first few weeks will be helpful to the learning process.

Use your signal. All of us need a warning before we can be expected to perform in unison. At a track meet, the words "ready" and "set" precede "go!" Before a play begins, the lights are dimmed and a tone is sounded a few times. On the street, a yellow light warns of the soon-coming red. So it is with an effective Attention Signal. Students need to know that their attention is about to be required. This gives them time to make a quick mental transition to the next behavior expectation. One common example is to simply hold up your hand with five fingers extended (visual cue). Put down one finger per second while you audibly announce the following: "I will need your attention in five . . . four . . . (give a social cue) . . . three . . . two . . . (give a second social cue) . . . one." Other examples include a chime, train whistle, or taped music. Many lower grade teachers will use this rhyme: "One, two, three . . .

eyes on me." In these classes, students are taught to chorally respond with their own rhyme: "One . . . two . . . eyes on you." Others use the "shave and a haircut" clapping pattern, with the students providing the last two claps.

Eye contact. When the five-second warning period has elapsed, pause just long enough to make eye contact with every student. This takes only seconds, but it is very important. The pause for eye contact signals that you are serious about requiring each person's attention. It gives you the time you need to ensure that you have it. This is also the accountability check to ensure that every student is attending to you.

This step is as easy as it sounds. From your position in the front of the class, sweep your eyes over the class from one side to the other, making contact with each student along the way. Each contact can take one second or less. Employ a mild corrective procedure when you find a student who is not attending. When you are finished, simply say thank you.

Social cues. After you have given the attention signal, monitor the class for compliance. As you see students clearing their desks and giving you eye contact, point out two or three who are doing it the right way. For example, "Good job, Matt." "Thank you, Jennifer." "I know Table 2 is ready because their table is clear and everyone has their protective goggles on." "I've got everyone in this row with their books out and looking forward." Statements like these not only reinforce the desired behavior, but they remind other students what is expected. Ask yourself, "What do I want this to look/sound like?" Only two or three of these cues are necessary to make a difference. (See Strategy 1.)

Begin immediately. Attention can be flighty. It is easily lost when students have nothing to do . . . such as waiting for the teacher to begin. Teachers who make the effort to get everyone's attention but then fail to begin immediately have wasted that time and effort. Even worse, they teach their class that they are not really serious when they ask for attention. In every shift of attention there is a very brief moment that punctuates the transition from one activity to another. It is into that critical moment that you must quickly leap if you are to maintain the attention of your class. Watch for it. You can feel it, almost sense it. To allow that critical moment to pass is to set yourself up for behavior problems. To employ it to your advantage is to set the stage for a productive lesson.

STRATEGY 3 ▶ Use Self-Starters

Always have a task for students to begin working on, even during the brief time between entering the room and starting the day's lesson. Once students have entered your classroom, they have two choices: 1) continue to behave as if they were in the chaos of the hall or playground, or 2) change their behavior by getting right to work. Assuming you want them to choose the latter option, you need to have a task for them to immediately begin working on when they arrive.

These tasks are often referred to as "bell work" (the work students are doing when the bell rings) or "self-starters" (work students can start without direction from the teacher). Students learn that when they enter the room they are to hang up their coats, move quickly to their seats, and begin working on a self-starter. This way, students who choose to be in the classroom have also chosen to begin working on a self-starter. Those who want to continue socializing must remain outside the class. At the moment the bell rings, every student should be in his or her seat quietly working.

It is all too common to see students enter the room running around, laughing, pushing, and talking loudly, just as they were doing during the class change or elementary recess. This places an unnecessary burden on the teacher. When I watch new teachers taking roll and gathering their materials for the day amid all of this disorder, I feel sorry for them. Tolerating

Essential Components of Self-Starters

- Directions and materials for assignment are ready to go before students enter the room.

- Assignment is designed to be completed in 5–10 minutes.

- Most students are at or near the fluent level on the content of the assignment.

- Work is turned in, but only a sampling of materials corrected.

this behavior makes the job of establishing order all that much more difficult. They also lose the chance to create a sense that their classroom is a place for learning, not playing.

Teachers who do not use a self-starter must begin from scratch when they call students to order and begin their lesson. How much easier it is to gain student attention when students are already in their seats working quietly!

At a minimum, there should be bell work at the beginning of every day. It is most useful to teachers when they provide it every time students enter the classroom. The purpose of self-starters is behavioral, not academic. This means that the content should be material that students have already mastered to a level of fluency that they are almost guaranteed to be able to complete it successfully. It should be designed to last only about 5 to 10 minutes, although students who arrive early will have more time to complete it. It should be posted on the board in the same place every day so that students can get right to work without teacher direction. It could be a review of material already learned or a new but simple task on which students can practice previously mastered skills. When used at the beginning of the day, this is also a time for you to take roll and attend to those minor but inevitable administrative duties.

It is important to remind students of the procedure. "When you enter the room please pick up a quarter sheet of paper that you will find here, then quickly take your seat. As soon as you sit down, look at the board for today's self-starter and get right to work." After greeting the students, the teacher moves to the back of the room for two minutes to monitor students as they begin. Then the teacher moves around the room offering quiet social cues. (See Strategy 1.) When the class is fully engaged, the teacher can then take roll and tend to business tasks.

Guidelines and Examples

Here are a few guidelines for designing your bell work:

Keep it simple. Students should recognize that they can complete it successfully and quickly. If the task is too challenging, they will avoid starting as long as possible.

Have any necessary materials readily available. This could be a paper placed on each desk in advance, a box with newspaper clippings ready to be picked up, or a quote written on the board in advance.

Don't give yourself an extra stack of papers to grade. Some teachers simply go through the stack of papers and record that the work was completed. Some correct only a random sampling. Some have a student record who has and has not turned in their work. The purpose here is to start students working, not grade their performance. (In middle school, class points can be given for completion.)

EXAMPLES:

▶ Write on the board four recall questions from yesterday's history lesson for students to answer.

▶ Give students a 1" x 2" newspaper clipping and have them circle all of the letters m, x, and w.

▶ Write three sentences on the board with grammatical errors in them. Have students copy the sentences exactly and then make the necessary corrections on their paper.

▶ Write three math problems from last week's lesson on the board.

▶ Have students write a daily paragraph in their journal on the topic posted in the room.

▶ Post a mind bender or word game on the board for students to solve.

▶ Have students list the most unusual uses for a fork they can think of.

STRATEGY 4 ▶ Proximity Control

Classroom management is not such a big issue for tutors or teachers working with small groups. All of those students get front-row seats. It's when there are two or more rows that student attention suffers and on-task behavior begins to slide. In our pubic school classrooms that hold as many as 30 to 35 students, the physical proximity of the teacher becomes a major tool in managing classroom behavior. In fact, some would argue that the physical distance between the teacher's body and the student is the single most important factor governing the likelihood of students goofing off in the classroom.

REFLECTION QUESTION

In my classroom, who is giving me the greatest attention, students in the front of the class or those in the back?

In your first two decades of life, you spent most of your waking time in classrooms. You already know how it works. If the teacher is not paying attention to what you are doing, you can fiddle with other things, visit with your neighbor, or simply daydream. If there are rows of heads and shoulders separating you from the teacher, he or she can't see what you are doing. If you simply blend into the back of the crowd, the odds are that you will not be called on or even noticed. You are free to do whatever you care to do.

Understanding the relationship between proximity and student behavior is a powerful tool in managing student behavior in your classroom. The skills of proximity control are the same skills used by singers, comedians, preachers, and politicians to connect with the crowd. Teachers who teach from behind a podium or desk assure the students in the back rows that they can goof off with very little risk of being caught. Teachers who are exclusively tied to the whiteboard or an overhead projector unintentionally grant a "free parking" pass to students in the back half of the room. Teachers who sit at their desk correcting papers while students are supposed to be quietly doing seatwork are asking for trouble. Teachers who always teach from the same location have unknowingly contributed to their own classroom management problems.

Strategy 4 is as simple as it is important: move frequently throughout your classroom to constantly create new "front rows" of student attention.

These changing zones of high-intensity supervision sharply reduce opportunities for students to goof off. Knowing the teacher is approaching or will soon approach them increases the risk that they will be caught talking to

Essential Components of Proximity Control

- Move around the room during seatwork, lectures, demonstrations, group work, or overhead presentations.

- Constantly create new "front rows" of student attention.

- Do not sit at your desk when the class is present.

a friend, playing with stuff, passing notes, or just daydreaming. They know the odds, so they stop.

Moving constantly through the room when the class is doing seatwork is a natural way to intervene when the class is being chatty or some disruptive behavior is going on, but it is actually much more important than that. It is a critical way to *prevent* chatty and disruptive behavior. When the class is quietly working, your constantly changing proximity is your tool to maintain this behavior. Be sure that the arrangement of desks in your room does not take away your ability to use this strategy. You must be able to easily move to within eight feet of any student. (See Strategy 6.)

So what can you do while you are moving? You can do nearly everything that you do when you are stationary in the front of the class. You can lecture and give directions on the move. You can look over students' shoulders to check for understanding. You can address individual questions and concerns in a whisper without disrupting the concentration of everyone else. You can provide a quiet redirection if it is needed. (See Strategies 17 and 18.) You can monitor the work of small groups and learning centers. You can reinforce good work and following directions with quiet praise.

One of my fourth grade teachers used an overhead projector instead of writing on the whiteboard. That gave her the ability to always face the class as she was teaching—a great idea. However, she rarely moved from the front and center position next to the projector. The students picked right up on this pattern, so those students in the back corners of the room had the lowest engagement rate in the class. The odds of being caught were almost nil. The teacher rarely noticed them and they knew it. After this was pointed out to her, she was able to quickly solve the problem by spending more time teaching from the back of the room. She could still use the overhead. However, by teaching from various places around the room, she was able to quickly and easily improve her student engagement rate.

Here's another example that came from a seventh grade science class. A new teacher had wonderful and well-prepared lessons, all of which she delivered from behind a large demonstration table in front of the whiteboard. That table served as a fence between the class and the teacher. Even the front row was distant! When students became chatty and disruptive, she would issue missiles of verbal corrections, threats, and sarcastic put-downs to control behavior. When we suggested that she teach from the aisles instead of from behind that huge science table and use a few social cues while doing so, things turned around very quickly. Proximity became her primary tool of prevention. Because her lessons were already very good, she needed little else.

Successful teachers simply do not have time to sit at their desk or tie themselves to the front of the room when their class is present. Proximity control is too important a management strategy to discard.

STRATEGY 5 ▶ Time Limits

You have a plan when you start class. You want your students to complete their work so that you can move on with your plan. There is a lot to do today. Time is of the essence. Your students, on the other hand, have settled into another long assignment . . . just like every other day. To them, there is no reason to hurry. I'll just take my time, stretch it out, visit with my neighbor, time to kick back. As the seemingly endless assignment drags on, their attention drifts. Soon you and the students are at odds. Your orderly class begins to fray, as does your patience.

REFLECTION QUESTION

Do my students think they have time to kick back?

Time is your most important resource. We typically have only 180 days of school for our students to learn a fully packed curriculum. Deduct from that

Essential Components of Time Limits

- Post the schedule for the day's lesson.

- Announce a clear time limit for each assignment.

- Use a timer or a watch.

- Incorporate "wait time."

lunches, recesses, taking roll, school assemblies, transitioning activities, various emergency drills, parent conferences, distributing materials, cleaning up, holiday parties and events, and there is very little time left to do justice to the curriculum. Now, deduct even deeper into what little remains the time it takes for you to correct misbehavior in your classroom, and both you and your students have been badly short-changed.

Time itself can also be a constructive ally if you use it to your advantage. It can motivate, keep students engaged and on task, and keep activities fresh and interesting for another day. The careful measurement of time can be a tool to prevent disruptions and confrontations. Time constraints help anchor students in the moment. Knowing how much time is allocated to a task and how much time remains gives students the opportunity to learn how to manage their own time and the pace of their work.

"Here's today's schedule." Post the schedule of tasks for the day's lesson with a time limit for each task. This will serve as a road map for the lesson (and, for your more reluctant learners, provide the light at the end of the tunnel). The lesson schedule can be posted each day in a regular designated space on the whiteboard. Not only does it help students to organize their thinking about what is ahead but it also helps you to stay on task as well. Middle school teachers will want to post a schedule for each prep. Elementary teachers will only post the schedule for the major subjects. A posted schedule fosters self-discipline for both students and teachers. It also communicates to the class that there is a plan, their teacher is organized, and she knows what she is doing.

"Time's up in one minute." By announcing a clear time limit on the task to be completed, you will not only keep your plan on track, you will improve on-task behavior. Be sure that you don't give them too much time. Class time spent waiting means trouble for the teacher. If your students have 20 minutes to complete a seatwork assignment, tell them. Even more important, give them a five-minute warning before their time is up. Then mean it. On the minute of the deadline, have them put away their work and begin the transition to the next task. Use time limits for short tasks as well as longer projects. Remember, if you say it, mean it. Sticking to your time limits tells the student that when the teacher says something, he or she means it.

Examples of "Time's Up" Alerts for Grades 3–5:

▶ "I will need your eyes on me in 10 seconds . . . 5 . . . 4 . . . 3 . . . 2 . . . 1."

▶ "I want everyone to think of an answer to the next question. I will give you six seconds to think before we start. When you have thought of an answer, hold up your little finger." [Use *thumb* for older grades.]

▶ "You now need to put away your work and clean up your area. We also need someone to clean up the clutter by the sink and under the coat rack. I will give you four minutes to get ready, and then you can go to recess. Ready . . . begin."

Examples of "Time's Up" Alerts for Grades 6 and Up:

▶ "You have one minute to return to your seats, take out your notebooks and a pencil, and give me your eyes."

▶ "Your group will have 15 minutes to complete this task. When your time is up, we will draw for the first group to report out. I will give you a two-minute warning."

▶ "I need to see everyone in their seats and beginning their assignment in 40 seconds."

Use a timer or watch. Many teachers use a timer for two purposes: 1) to help stay organized and on schedule and 2) to signal the class when it is time to move on to the next task. The timer, then, becomes the fair and predictable reason we ran out of time, not the teacher's mood on that day. The timer is the third-party arbitrator of what we do and when we do it. A watch or large clock in the classroom can accomplish the same function. The teacher makes an obvious show of looking at his watch or the clock on the wall. Some teachers will write on the board the ending time for the 20-minute assignment. Students know these teachers really mean business when they say, "You have 15 minutes to complete this task" and then set the timer.

"Wait Time." Here is a surprisingly common classroom scenario. The teacher asks a question. Two or three hands shoot up. The teacher calls on one student who immediately gives the correct answer. The teacher moves on, believing that this is evidence that all of the students now understand the concept being taught. Trouble is, they don't.

In fact, the situation is even worse than the students simply not understanding the concept. Behavior problems begin to pop up. Students in these classes quickly learn that they are excused from participating in this kind of class discussion because someone else will always satisfy the teacher with a correct answer. In fact, they learn that they don't even have to listen to the questions anymore. They can doodle, whisper, talk, and play around as much as they like, as long as they don't draw the notice of the teacher.

In 1972, Mary Rowe came up with the notion of "wait time." She found that when teachers would wait three or more seconds before calling on a student, more students participated, the quality of their responses improved, and test scores went up. Those few seconds gives everyone a chance to mentally restate the question, think of an answer, and, in so doing, process what the teacher had just said. Because the teacher had given everyone time to think of an answer, hands are not necessary. The teacher can call on anyone in the class to answer. Because there is now a chance that they will be called on, more students participate. Further, when the teacher calls on several students for an answer instead of being satisfied with only one, the teacher is getting valuable feedback on the level of understanding in the classroom. (See Strategy 12.)

By using wait time, this is how our classroom scenario would now look. The teacher asks a question and tells the class that she will give them five seconds to think of the answer. She looks at her watch. When the time is up, she randomly calls on four students. "Eva, what did you come up with?" Eva answers, but the teacher does not respond. "Matty, what about you?" Again, Matty gives his answer but the teacher does not respond, even if it is the same as Eva's. "Leila, what were your thoughts?" Leila responds with the wrong answer, but the teacher does not correct it. "Ben, what was your answer?" Ben gives the correct answer. The teacher then goes on to confirm the correct answer and review why it is correct. No one is singled out. Everyone participates by having at least thought of an answer, even if they were not called upon to share it. The teacher has conducted a random check for understanding and received some valuable insight into the classes' level of understanding. Even better, there is no down time giving students the chance to misbehave.

STRATEGY 6 ▶ Seating Arrangements

There are many ways to arrange desks in a classroom, but these arrangements have only two implications for teachers. Some allow teachers to move around the room, and some restrict teacher movement. In your classroom, pick the first type. The effectiveness of the skill of proximity control depends upon your fluid movement around the classroom. (See Strategy 4.)

One of my new teachers set up her second grade classroom in five horizontal rows of six with no aisles. During both lessons and seatwork, she was able to move only around the perimeter of the class. Students on the front and sides always got the "front row" seats, but students in the middle never did. Consequently, there was always a buzz of off-task conversation and fiddling in the room, led by the children located in the middle. The arrangement of the desks kept her from any close contact with those children. Simple solution: break up the long rows with two aisles. Having five rows with two plus two plus two across enabled her to use the strategy of proximity control.

With so many variables in teaching styles, physical space limitations, class size, student age and maturity, and instructional designs, there is not one ideal classroom arrangement. Each teacher needs to develop his or her own preference. The good news is that you also have the ability to periodically try out some different arrangements. Not only do these give you the opportunity to test out other possibilities, but a new arrangement can also serve as a helpful change of pace for the students. This strategy addresses several considerations in developing a seating arrangement for your class.

Assign seating. The best practice is to assign seating. Most teachers do. It's your classroom and you are in charge. It certainly makes memorizing student names easier. As you get to know your students, you will want to make adjustments in seat assignments to separate problem students. Students who require a lot of supervision should be seated close to the front of the room. Those who work well independently can be seated in the back corners. Students with visual or auditory disabilities should be seated where they can best see or hear you. It doesn't take long to figure out that some students should not be sitting next to each other. As this becomes evident, the corrective action is clear: separate them. Dr. Ginger Rhode (1994) says it this way: "Having tough kids sit together is like disruptive behavior ability grouping."

Teacher access. Be sure you can easily move within eight feet of any student for proximity control. Arrange the desks or tables in a pattern that enables you to stand next to every student in the room. Select or devise an arrangement with wide aisles where you can walk without tripping over student feet or bumping into backpacks hung from the back of a chair. Be sure that there are enough aisles to allow you to easily reach anyone.

Essential Things to Consider in Classroom Seating Arrangements

- Teacher-assigned seating, with consideration for students with special needs.

- Teacher can easily move within eight feet of any student for proximity control.

- No student has his or her back to the front of the room.

- Table or chairs are set for small-group instruction (teacher facing center of room).

- One student desk is designated for "seat away."

- A carpet can be used in lower grades for whole-class instruction.

- A classroom computer needs to have access to outlets and lines.

- Teacher's desk is out of the way.

- Calm the room through staging.

- Try out several arrangements.

Facing forward. Students should have a clear line of sight to the front of the room, either by facing the front or by looking down the center of a cluster of desks. Because you will want eye contact with every student, no one should be sitting with his or her back to the front.

Small groups. In elementary schools, include in your floor plan space for a table or a semicircle of five to seven chairs set for small-group instruction, with your chair set to face the center of the room for supervision.

Seat away. Have one student desk designated for "seat away." This is a place for a disruptive student to immediately move to until you have time to meet individually with him or her. (See Strategy 18.)

Lower-grade carpets. Lower-grade teachers will often use a carpet on which younger children can sit during whole-group instruction, story reading, or sharing.

Classroom computer. In some schools you will need a desk or a table designed for a classroom computer(s). Placement of this equipment may be largely dictated by proximity to outlets and necessary cables.

Teacher desk. Place your desk in a location that does not interfere with your instructional area and does not inhibit your ability to move around the classroom. You will not be using it very much while class is in session.

Calm the room through staging. Occasionally, a little change in the atmosphere of the room will keep it fresh and build anticipation for what is to follow. Even if the task is completely familiar, a minor adjustment in the environment in which students are working can generate interest and engagement. Several examples are listed below:

- Have soft classical or other instrumental music playing softly in the background.

- Turn off the florescent lights and use a few less caustic lamps instead while teaching from an overhead projector.

- Place a few live plants around the room.

- Turn out the lights and have a video related to the lesson playing as students enter and take their seats.

- Place a thickly upholstered chair or couch in the room for you to use in story reading or students to use in a reading corner.

- Bring in a carpet for students to sit on when you conduct a class discussion or read a story.

- Display a few posters of calming, natural scenes.

Try out several arrangements. It is not necessary to keep the same seating arrangement for an entire school year. Three or four different arrangements in the course of a year give students a refreshing perspective on their work. They give you a chance to see which arrangements best suit your instructional style. The variety will also create different combinations of student groups and neighbors.

Seating Arrangement Ideas

▲ In the Appendix (pages 141–144) you will find several possible seating arrangements and brief explanations.

STRATEGY 7 ▶ Manage Your Transitions

When your students change from one task to another, you probably feel more vulnerable than at any other point in your school day. That's because you are. You have some students who are ready to go as soon as you suggest it is time to move, others who didn't quite hear you because they are still so focused on the previous activity, still others who don't quite understand what you are asking them to do, and then there are the few who see this as a chance to visit and stretch and see what else is going on around the room. You end up cajoling, correcting, and confronting to regain attention and redirect their focus to the new activity. A transition that should take less than a minute ends up consuming three to five, and you find yourself spending more energy on managing misbehavior than on teaching.

I worked with a high school science teacher who would transition from lecture to seatwork by personally passing out a worksheet to each student in the class. He would provide instructions for completing the worksheet after every student had received one. Students obviously had a lot of down time waiting not only to receive their paper but also waiting

Essential Components of Managing Transitions

- Be prepared.

- Use your attention signal.

- Explain what you now want them to do and the time allocated to do it, holding students in their seats until you give the signal to proceed.

- Provide an opportunity for students to ask questions.

- Check for understanding.

- Give a signal to begin. Provide two to three social cues.

- Give a five-second warning.

- Use your attention signal to begin the next activity.

for his instructions. This, then, was their time to visit with each other, text their friends, leave their seats, take out homework for another class, or put their head down for a quick nap. When the teacher was finally ready to give the instructions, it was a struggle to regain the attention of the class. Worse, he had set the stage to turn that science class into a social event.

Initially, transitions need to be highly structured. When students begin to handle transitions comfortably as a routine procedure, some of the initial structure may be relaxed. The sequence for managing a transition outlined below has been useful for many successful teachers.

Be prepared. Do not attempt a transition to another activity or task unless you are completely prepared for that activity or task to begin immediately.

Use your attention signal. Be sure you have the attention of the class before you begin any instructions. (See Strategy 2.)

Explain what you want them to do. As soon as you begin explaining what to do next, some students will begin to move. It is important that they remain in their seats until you signal them to move. This gives you the chance to complete your instructions and check for understanding. Include in your instructions the amount of time they have to complete the transition.

Provide an opportunity for students to ask questions. Allow only a few questions. The ones that emerge first are most likely to be pertinent for the others.

Check for understanding. Ask two or three students to repeat portions of your instructions. "Sam, what are we going to work on next?" "Brianna, where are you going to move?" "Sarah, how much time do you have to get there?"

Give a signal to begin. When you think they are clear about what is to happen next, give a signal to begin the transition. Be obvious in watching the clock or looking at your watch. As the students move, use two or three social cues to remind them about your expectations. (See Strategy 1.)

Give a five-second warning. Calmly tell the students when they have five seconds to begin the next task.

Use your attention signal to begin the next activity. When the time is up, use your attention signal once again and move quickly into the next activity.

OTHER CONSIDERATIONS

Transitions can be tough. Besides these essential components, there are a few other considerations that may help if you are finding difficulty in your transitions.

Take time to settle after recess. Re-entry after recess can be a particularly challenging time for an elementary teacher. They come running in hot and sweaty, loudly using their recess voices, pushing and jostling just as they were doing on the playground. You can save the time and energy it takes to settle them down by inserting a brief procedure between recess and class work.

- Instruct your students that when the bell rings, they are to line up before coming in. They can line up at a designated place on the playground, in the hall outside of the classroom, or along the outside wall of the classroom. Before they enter the classroom, however, you must be present to invite them in after they have settled down.

- While they are still in line, this is a great time for you to remind your students what they are to do when they enter the room or give them directions for the next task they will be working on. When you have determined they are ready to re-enter your classroom, direct them to enter the class quietly and get right to work. With this very brief intervention, you can better preserve the productive climate you have worked so hard to create in your classroom.

- Use a self-starter activity. (See Strategy 3.)

Transition from class to special project or activity. There are times when we ask students to change their mind-set from an academic setting, in which they may passively sit under the teacher's direction, to a more active project setting, in which they are expected to be self-directed and personally responsible. If students are not prepared for that shift, they waste time wandering or waiting to be told what to do next. While still in a passive setting, have them write down two things before they move to the lab, gym, shop, kitchen, or an activity center. First, what is the first thing they will work on when they get there? Second, have them write down what they will do if someone else is using the equipment they need. Turning in this quarter sheet of paper is their "ticket" to go to work.

REFLECTION QUESTION

What gives me the most trouble during transitions?

Transition Ideas

Try these tips for making transitions flow smoothly:

▲ Be sure your materials for the next activity are ready.

▲ Give a warning that a transition is about to occur.

▲ "Advertise" the next activity to make it sound fun and exciting, something they would be eager to start.

▲ Keep your instructions simple. Try numbering them, "First . . ., second. . ., then third . . ."

▲ Prepare an attention grabber to start the new activity.

▲ Take great care to eliminate as much wait time as possible. Avoid having students wait for stragglers by allowing them to start the next activity while you individually attend to the stragglers.

▲ For some activities, try conducting your transition with small groups to reduce confusion. ("As I call your table number, you can put down your pencils. Then the person seated closest to the door can pick up the directions and the equipment your group will need for the experiment. Until your group is called, I want you to continue working on your assignment.")

▲ Use a sensory cue for routine transitions (warning bell, taped music, flicked lights, whispered warning to each small group).

STRATEGY 8 ▶ Teach Classroom Rules and Procedures

Every effective discipline program begins with the same assumption: that the students know and understand your expectations. We need to challenge this assumption. What is the specific behavior we are expecting from our students, and how do they know?

Expectations usually come in the form of class rules posted conspicuously in the classroom. They must be specific, observable, and stated in positive terms. They are explained, modeled, prompted, rehearsed, and periodically reviewed. Experienced teachers often include a "compliance rule" to cover situations for which there is not a rule. (Example: "Follow teacher directives the first time.") Your list of rules should be short, five or fewer, because a few rules are much more likely to be remembered.

> ### Essential Components of Teaching Rules and Procedures
>
> - Clearly state your expectations in five or fewer rules.
>
> - Make them specific, observable, and worded in positive terms.
>
> - Explicitly teach them (explain, model, prompt, and review).

We can't hold students accountable for what they have not been taught. Students need to know exactly what it looks and sounds like when they are meeting your expectations. Post your rules, then teach them. Teaching rules involves explaining what you mean, providing examples and non-examples, and referring to them each day or two at the beginning of the year to emphasize their importance. From time to time you will need to revisit the posted rules to teach them again, along with the reasons they are important. On occasion you may find a need to replace a rule as a means of addressing an issue that has come up in your class. This works fine if the new rule is explicitly taught just as the others were.

The teacher makes the final decision about the rules to be followed in a particular class. While students can question the rules as they are being taught or reviewed, the rest of the time they stand as posted. No further discussion. Any decision to change an unduly strict rule is made solely by the teacher.

Teaching rules. Rules are taught just like lessons are taught: explain, model, prompt, review (Brinkman and Williams, 2005).

EXPLAIN. Start with an explanation (this is my expectation, what I mean by it, and why it is important for us). Make sure to state what your expectation looks like and what it sounds like. To check for understanding, call on students to restate the rule or the reasons for having it.

MODEL. Show or describe some examples and non-examples (i.e., the right way and the wrong way). Elementary teachers may want to have the students role-play what it looks like and what it doesn't look like. Rehearse the behavior to firm the concept. ("I want you to go out into the hallway and re-enter the class, this time taking your seats and beginning work on

Sample Rules

▲ Some teachers will create a process to allow students to help establish the rules. This can be a good idea, but it may be unnecessarily cumbersome for the beginning teacher. I recommend establishing your own rules. On pages 47 and 48, you will find a sampling of rules for both elementary and middle school classrooms, from which you might select (or adapt) four or five.

the self-starter just like we discussed," or, "When I tell you to, make a little conversational buzz. Then listen for my attention signal.") You might also want to point out examples of what worked in the past and what did not, drawing from real classes or events.

PROMPT/CUE. Use a word, signal, or phrase to alert students to the rule. ("Remember to use only six-inch voices when you start your group work." "Today I will be watching for students who remember to keep their hands to themselves.") Social cues serve the dual purpose of cueing the rule and reinforcing compliance (see Strategy 1). You will need to use more at the first of the year, but the need to use them periodically will continue throughout the year.

REVIEW & REFINE. It is important that you do not make exceptions for a rule, if it is to become a habit. Periodically you will need to revisit or refine a rule by re-explaining and/or re-rehearsing it. ("I can see that we have forgotten the rule about showing respect to others. Let's take a few minutes to look at that rule again.") For the first two weeks of school, a review of all or some of the rules should be conducted daily at the beginning of the class.

Examples of Rules for Grades 3–5:

KHFOOTY (Keep Hands, Feet, and Other Objects to Yourself)

Use only six-inch voices when working in groups.

Show respect for other people.

Take responsibility for your actions.

Follow teacher directions the first time.

Keep our classroom clean.

Do not take out trinkets or toys in class.

Examples of Rules for Grades 6 and Up:

Show respect for other people.

Offensive words are not allowed.

Arrive in class on time.

Raise your hand and wait to be called on if you need assistance or have a question.

Be in your seat when the bell rings.

Ask permission before leaving the class, then use the hall pass.

CHAPTER 3

Positive Relationships:

CARE, TRUST, AND RESPECT

• • •

Effective classrooms are those in which the students believe the teacher knows them personally and cares about them. The rooms have an atmosphere of respect. They are productive, organized, and focused on learning. Robert Marzano found that the percentile decrease in disruptions was 50 points lower in middle school classrooms, 45 points lower in upper elementary classes, and 21 points lower in high school classrooms characterized by a positive student-teacher relationship when compared to classrooms that lacked this positive relationship. (Marzano, 2003).

Teachers in these classrooms carefully establish a balance point between authority and friendliness. Too much of either will tip the scale and have a negative effect on the behavior of the class. Excessive focus on rules and consequences creates resentment and subversion. Excessive efforts to befriend students leads to a loss of respect and weakened teacher authority and control. This balance point, then, is the definition of a positive relationship between teachers and students. Where this positive relationship exists, students are more likely to accept your rules and procedures, as well as the consequences when there is a violation.

The first impression you create as students enter your room can have a great effect on their behavior once they are inside. Each time students enter the room, the stage is set for whatever is to follow. If the environment feels positive as they enter, they are much more likely to see that day's lesson in a positive light. If it feels negative and oppressively controlled, the lesson will be unpleasant for them and, eventually, for you. Your classroom is a learning environment, not an extension of the playground, mall, home, or neighborhood. By preparing for their entry into the classroom, you seize the power to influence their attitude about you and your class and their expectations about what they are about to do. Developing a positive relationship starts on the first day and in the first minutes of class. This chapter describes three strategies for building positive relationships with your students.

"There are three things that you'll never find in a successful student-teacher interaction: purposeful humiliation, embarrassment, and a condescending tone. They force a hurtful and incorrect hierarchy, elevating the teacher to a higher position only by lowering the student. This is what bullies do, not teachers."

(Wormeli, 2003, p. 175)

STRATEGY 9 ▶ Show That You Care

When we care about someone and they care about us, we form a positive relationship. These positive relationships are extremely valuable to us— valuable enough, in fact, that we try very hard to protect them. So it is with the relationship between teachers and students. When students feel that their teacher cares about them as individuals, not just bodies in a classroom, it is difficult to be disrespectful or disruptive. To do so would jeopardize a valued relationship. What better position for a teacher to be in: his or her students choosing not to misbehave, even when they could!

How do you develop this kind of relationship? The same way we develop relationships with our friends. We know their names and use them frequently. We find common interests and converse about them. We share experiences with each other. We smile frequently. We are good listeners and show our genuine interest in what they have to say.

When it is personal, when they know something about you as a real person and you show your interest in them as real people, it is much more difficult for them to risk hurting you by being disruptive. It is also much more difficult for you to hurt them by losing your composure. In contrast, when you institutionalize yourself, act as if their thoughts and feelings are of no consequence to you, base your relationships only on rules and consequences, fail to seek or consider

Essential Ways to Show You Care

- Smile often.

- Use names.

- Share a laugh.

- Notice your students.

- Greet your students at the door.

- Be the teacher, not the peer.

their point of view, then disrupting the teacher's lesson will present no difficulty to them at all.

Make a point to show them that you are the kind of teacher who cares. Find occasions to share, listen, and laugh with them. Talk with them at recess, lunch, or before school. Seek their assistance and advice. Be personable.

Smile often. This is such a simple act, but it means so much. It communicates many positive things. A smile expresses satisfaction and reinforces desired behavior. It shows you to be friendly and approachable. It tells others that you are pleased with where you are and what you are doing. It portrays confidence and control, even in the face of disruptive behavior. Even when reviewing classroom rules and correcting misbehavior, a smile costs nothing yet buys you much.

Use names. Nothing speaks more loudly to us than hearing our own name. Use the power of this truth to your advantage by stating student names in a positive one-liner about them. It is not necessary to say something positive about every student every day, but it *is* necessary to be sure that no one is left out over the course of a week. For an assortment of reasons, some students need more positive comments than others. It's OK to be generous with them, as long as you are also genuine. These one-liners might sound something like this:

▶ "Good morning, Jackie. Good to see you today."

▶ "Welcome to school, Toby. Hope you have a great day."

▶ "Nice work on yesterday's assignment, Daniel."

▶ "Give me five, Megan."

▶ "Thanks, Mark, for getting right to work today."

▶ "Hey Travis."

▶ "What's up, Kayden."

Share a laugh. "Laughing and learning are the foundation of all successful long-term relationships" (Glasser, 1998, p. 41). William Glasser told us that laughter is magic. Sharing a laugh with students magically builds relationships faster than anything else. Laughing with a group is an affirmation of membership and acceptance in that group. Take a minute and tell a humorous story or anecdote while you wait two minutes for the bell to ring. Share a favorite cartoon, then post it in the room. Punctuate a lesson with a funny expression. Your students have plenty of jokes to tell as well. Invite two or three each day to tell one of their favorites (of course, with the obvious limitations).

Notice your students. Students who believe their teacher cares about them personally are far more likely to be compliant than those who see their teacher more as a controlling guard than a caring adult. Noticing something about your students is one of the ways we develop that positive relationship. There are many opportunities to notice your students. For example, make use of that informal period of time when they are just entering the room and settling down to task. Make a brief comment when you see them in the hall or lunchroom or whisper one as you walk around the room during seatwork. A simple statement spoken in a friendly tone is all that is needed.

▶ "Like your haircut, TJ."

▶ "Wow, Mike, you have a new backpack. I like it!"

▶ "Saw you at the soccer game last Saturday, Kayla."

▶ "You're always smiling, Scott. You make me want to smile, too."

▶ "Thanks, Erica, for helping with your group on that science project. It turned out great."

Greet your students at the door. Simply stand in the doorway as students enter the room and greet them. This method brings you bonus benefits. First, it is a subtle but effective way to establish a positive first impression for the day. Second, when several teachers are using this method together, it has a calming effect on student behavior in the hallway.

Consider how you were greeted the last time you entered a commercial aircraft, a car dealership, or a restaurant. Someone was standing in or by the doorway to greet you with a smile. Try this out on your own class. As you stand there, make eye contact with each student as she or he enters the room, give each a big smile, make a personal connection (e.g., high-five, shake hands, thumbs-up, bump fists, use their name), and welcome them to your class today. While this is a good thing to do daily, even using this strategy intermittently will help keep your students' impressions positive and personal.

> "Stand at the classroom door with a big smile and a ready handshake."
>
> (Wong and Wong, 2001, p. 105)

Be the teacher, not the peer. While it is important to develop a positive relationship, it is just as important to remember that you are not a peer to your students. You know it and so do they. You are the teacher, the voice of authority whose responsibility it is to teach, maintain order, and mediate conflict. Some new teachers make the mistake of developing friendships more like a peer in their efforts to build positive relationships with their students. You cannot fulfill your responsibilities as a teacher if you project yourself as a peer.

That subtle distance between teacher and student is surprisingly important. You need it for your judgments and directives to be taken seriously. You need it so that the ebb and flow of relationships between your students are distinct from and not allowed to cloud the relationship you have with any child in your class. You need it in emergency situations, when children will immediately look to an unquestioned authority figure to give them the direction they need to respond safely. Your students need the confidence that you are in charge. They need to know that you have the authority, the ability, and the will to restore order when the safety of students is threatened.

I worked with a first-year fifth grade teacher who wanted her students to call her by her first name. She wore flip-flops to school, played with them at recess, and made too many compromises to their preferences in class. Behavior got worse as students began to feel that they now had the power to determine how the class should be run. When she stepped back and re-established a little more distance and unilateral authority, classroom behavior came back under control. This process took some time on her part, but there was a noticeable change in the atmosphere of the class.

You send a signal about your relationship through your name, your dress, and the way you act. Introducing yourself as "Mr.," "Miss," "Mrs.," or "Ms." clearly says that you are not another peer. Dressing professionally reinforces your status. Using your own vocabulary and language patterns, instead of those of your students, says that you are an adult, and this is the way professional adults talk. Being the teacher in the room and not just a grown-up peer is a critical prerequisite to strengthen your authority in managing the behavior of your class and establishing a sense of safety for your students.

STRATEGY 10 ▶ Build Trust

Next to parents, teachers are usually cited as the most important adult in the life of a child. You bear a huge responsibility. You are the model of an educated person. You are considered to be a moral leader in the community. You are entrusted to act as a parent while the child is under your supervision.

In the eyes of each child, you are the person who ensures his or her safety. You have access to very personal information that should not be shared with anyone else. You are the protector, the authority, the confidant, the mediator, the counselor. You know what is in the child's best interest and can be trusted to act accordingly, even if he or she is reluctant to obey. In an emergency, the student looks to you to calmly direct the class to safety. In the chaos of recess or lunch, the child looks to you to establish and maintain order.

Essential Elements of Building Trust

- If you say it, mean it.

- Be consistent.

- Be the professional.

This is a serious responsibility. It also conveys upon you both a formal and informal authority to command obedience. You start the year with that authority on the basis of your formal position as teacher. You will maintain that authority to the extent that you are able to build and maintain genuine trust with your students. Nothing has a greater influence on the behavior of your students than the relationship you develop with them. That relationship must be founded upon trust.

If you say it, mean it. This sounds so simple, but the number of times we parents violate it with our own children by using careless language is embarrassing. The corollary to this component is, "Be careful what you say." Students monitor what their teachers say very carefully. They are always checking us to see if our directive is a requirement, or merely a suggestion. Consider these examples:

▶ Teacher *says*: "Class, I need your attention now."
   Students *see* the teacher talking to an individual, gathering up her own materials, and erasing the chalkboard without even looking at the class.

▶ Teacher *says*: "If you don't settle down, you will lose 3 minutes of recess."
   Students *see* several students still talking and playing with stuff in their desk when the recess bell rings, yet the class goes to recess on time.

▶ Teacher *says*: "The next person to throw something in this room is going to the office."
   Students *see* someone throw a pencil, but it only leads to another scolding.

 In these examples, the teacher's instructions are clear. The only question is when they will be enforced. So the game begins. The teacher's directive is the first step in a chain of threatened consequences. When the teacher gets tired of the chain, he eventually blows up. If that blow-up is the signal he really means it and action will finally be taken, the students will now comply. In some classes, this can even feel like a spectator sport filled with drama, intrigue, and fast action.

The remedy is simple. To show that you really mean it, follow through promptly. If you can't follow through (or if you didn't really mean it), don't say it. Teachers who mean what they say and follow through promptly enjoy a high rate of student compliance. They also enjoy a high degree of student trust.

A word of caution: occasionally a new teacher will threaten something that he or she cannot deliver. (For example, the student is sent to the office, but the office simply sends him back to class. The student is directed to stay after school, but the student rides the bus.) Check before you make such statements. Be certain that you can deliver on what you say so that you really can mean it.

Be consistent. We develop rules and expectations to create an orderly class and to give our students predictability. Do yourself a favor: be consistent as you apply and enforce your expectations. It will literally save you hours of conflict and argument, not only with students but also with their parents.

Check out these three examples in which new teachers get themselves in trouble.

1. You expect students to raise their hand before you call on them. John, the brightest student in your class, calls out an answer to a question and you accept it. Oops, you just compromised the raising-hand-to-be-recognized rule. It is now clear to the class that sometimes this rule is important, and sometimes it isn't. In their minds, the only way to find out if it is important this time is to test it out to see which rule applies today.

2. You want students to remain in their seats unless given permission to leave them. Betty and Jose, two usually well-behaved students, leave their seats to get a drink but are not corrected. Lesson to the class: sometimes it is important to stay in your seat unless given permission, and sometimes it isn't.

3. The deadline for science fair projects is on Wednesday. Rulon brings his in the following Monday, and it is accepted without penalty. Sam's mom hears about this and is furious. She calls and complains that Sam could have received a better grade if he also had an extra weekend to work on it, as Rulon did.

In each of these examples, the actual rule in practice was that the teacher will decide each day for each student in each specific circumstance. That is way too much for you to take on! You don't have time to make hundreds of decisions each day about who can do what, when, where, and under which circumstances. Define your rules, post them, teach them, and stick by them. (See Strategy 8.)

When you consistently apply the rules, the students can predict your reaction before they misbehave. For the students, that predictability creates a sense of security, a reassurance that the teacher is fair and even-handed to all, a confidence that the teacher cares about me just as much as my neighbor. For *you*, that predictability means you no longer need to make so many decisions as you go. You can simply apply the rule the fits, and the matter is closed.

Certainly extenuating circumstances arise and accommodations become necessary (broken leg, non-readers, new to school, etc.). The strategy of consistency applies here as well. Given a similar set of circumstances, would you make the same accommodation? If the answer is yes, and the accommodation is seen by the students to be reasonable, consistency is still in place, and the strategy of building trust has not been compromised.

Be the professional. Just as with the medical or legal professions, ethical standards of conduct prohibit teachers from casually sharing personal information about our students. When a student overhears us sharing confidential information about other students, we have undermined our own trustworthiness. We have also violated the law.

STRATEGY 11 ▶ Show Respect

You are the teacher. You are expected to be in charge of your class. When you call the class to order, it is expected that they will be attentive to you. When you tell students to do something, it is expected that they will do it promptly and without objection. When they interact with each other, it is expected that they will treat each other with respect. These behaviors are essential for a learning environment that is orderly, safe, and academically productive.

Essential Components of Earning Respect

- Address students by name.

- Use "please" and "thank you."

- Use a calm, warm speaking voice.

- Smile.

- Avoid sarcasm.

- Be on time and be ready.

- Assume benevolence.

- Preserve student dignity.

But what if your students are not being respectful? The first thing to recognize is that we cannot control another person. The only thing we can really control is ourselves. Experience teaches us, however, that our behavior has a major influence on the behavior of our students. The behavior we choose makes a tremendous difference in the behavior our students choose to use in our classroom.

Writing about middle-level students, Rick Wormeli (2003) uses the term "respect points" to describe relationships as a proactive strategy for preventing discipline problems.

"When a student feels known and respected by the adult in charge, he's less likely to counter the adult's authority. We earn 'respect points' every time we affirm a student's efforts, give students respect, elevate them rather than ourselves, and sincerely reach out to them when they are troubled . . . . There's no room here for sarcasm or put-downs from the students or the teacher." (p. 39)

REFLECTION QUESTION

Do I lead by example? (Mahatma Gandhi said it best: "We must be the change we wish to see in the world.")

Address students by name. Use student names frequently. There is something deep inside us that recognizes our name above all others. It validates us as an individual, not simply a member of a crowd. It signals that we are important enough to be identified by name. To be respectful, it must be pronounced correctly and used in a friendly manner.

Use "please" and "thank you." Businesses in the service sector make a habit of using good manners. The polite treatment of customers is essential to their survival. We need to apply that principle in our classrooms. As teachers, we can simply direct students to do something, or we can incorporate the word "please" as a sign of respect. Similarly, "thank you" communicates the same respect that we have come to expect as adults. It shows appreciation for their efforts. It communicates that we recognize their good work or the respect they have shown us. Your frequent use of "please" and "thank you" supports the positive climate you are trying to build in your class.

Use a calm, warm speaking voice. Tone is so important in our language. Words spoken in anger communicate a completely different message than the same words spoken with kindness. A verbal exchange in which each party progressively speaks louder and more quickly tends to accelerate a confrontation. Words spoken in a calm manner communicate that we are in charge, we are confident, and that we know what we are doing. Even when a student is being blatantly disrespectful, a genuinely calm and controlled voice tends to ease the tension and defuse the situation. It communicates that we respect the student's point of view, even if we don't agree with it. It communicates the respect we expect to see our students give us when they disagree with our decisions.

Smile. A gracious host always has a smile for his or her guests. A kind smile costs so little, yet its impact on our relationships can be powerful. It communicates acceptance, appreciation, and understanding. Consider the power of this respectful correction: Approach a student who is talking to his neighbor. Smile (even if your impulse is to yell in front of the entire class). Calmly and quietly say, "Scott (pause until you have his attention). Please stop talking to Tyler and get back to work. Thank you, Scott." Slight smile, then return to monitoring your class.

Avoid sarcasm. Sarcasm is a counterproductive killer for your classroom environment. Not only does it communicate disrespect, it often finds humor at another's expense. If the teacher uses sarcasm, students believe themselves to be on shaky ground. Because they think they could well be the next victim, they lose respect for the teacher. More important, they also lose trust. (See Strategy 10.)

Be on time and be ready. Teachers who arrive late to class and unprepared to begin teaching certainly send the wrong signal to their students. Keeping others waiting is the height of disrespect for their valuable time. The way we model our respect for time is a lesson we teach our students each and every day, for better or worse.

Assume benevolence. Students will misbehave. That is a given. The way we react to their mistakes will teach them how they should react when others, in turn, offend them. If we assume that their offense was intentional and malicious, they will assume the same of their peers. On the other hand, if we assume that this was a simple mistake and give them a fair chance to explain what happened, we teach them lifelong principles of due process, justice, and fairness. By assuming benevolence in their actions, we teach them respect.

Preserve student dignity. A very powerful principle for teachers to remember is to preserve student dignity. Not to do so is to create even more problems. When that dignity is challenged in front of their peers, they have no choice but to resist you, either actively or passively. The likelihood that you will change student behavior rises when dignity and personal power are preserved. So how can you do this?

CHOICE. When correcting a student, you can offer a choice. That choice affords the student a form of control. It signals that you recognize he or she is capable of making good choices. It has the effect of transforming the student's state of mind from a framework that is emotional and reactive to one that is rational. When you provide a choice, you increase the odds of avoiding a power struggle.

DISTANCE. When a teacher gets into a student's face it is a form of aggression that accelerates power struggles. The student is more likely to respond with the intent of "getting even" than compliance. Interventions that preserve personal space usually prevent power struggles and confrontations. They give the student time to think, and they allow the student some latitude in deciding when to comply. ("I'll follow your directive when I decide to follow your directive.")

PRIVACY. Public ridicule is dangerous. Not only does it breed resentment in the student receiving it, it has a chilling effect on the rest of the class. Students who are more timid and quiet tend to become fearful that they will be corrected in front of the class. Other students will look for ways to get even. Relationships nearly always suffer. Certainly we will need to correct students in front of the class from time to time. But care must be taken so that students do not feel demeaned or ridiculed in the process.

CHAPTER 4

Instruction:

HARNESS THE POWER
OF AN INTERESTING LESSON

• • •

Young people are engines of energy. They constantly need to be actively engaged in something. They are predisposed to engagement. It is the way they explore their world and discover how to interact with it. It is also part of their charm, part of the reason that we choose to become their teachers. However, if we have nothing to engage our students' attention in our classrooms, they will certainly find something else on their own. They simply can't help it.

This is where we sometimes get in trouble. When they don't find our lesson engaging, they turn instead to something that is. They bring out their trinkets and toys, visit with a neighbor, giggle and push, doodle and draw, or invent new activities that will engage their young minds. For us, all of this is disruptive. For them, it is simply natural.

Our job is to direct this natural energy. Our goal is to have an average of 80% of the class engaged during instruction as well as seatwork (90% during a read-aloud activity). We are always seeking ideas that will engage students in our lessons. This would not be necessary if they were intrinsically interested in what we want them to learn. For example, their intrinsic interest in dinosaurs has made this a favorite unit for generations of young children. When students are engaged, their behavior is not a problem. So teachers have a strong incentive to teach dinosaurs because students find the subject so interesting.

Obviously not all subjects will build such a high level of interest in your classroom. In fact, most won't. But there are a number of strategies available to you that can foster student engagement in even the most drab of subjects. Using them gives us a 2-for-1 bonus: student learning goes up, behavior problems go down.

"Most discipline or classroom management issues boil down to disconnections between teacher practices and student needs."

(Wormeli, 2003, p. 34)

STRATEGY 12 ▶ Get Your Students Participating

Students are less likely to misbehave in an interesting lesson than in a boring lesson. No surprise there. However, this simple truism means that we need to pay some serious attention to building interest in our lessons. When your lessons are not engaging, it is unrealistic to expect your students to remain focused. I have worked with teachers who complain that they can't do a more exciting lesson until the students' behavior improves. This statement is a clear paradox. Their behavior will not improve because the lessons remain so dry.

The fastest way to build interest is to get students participating and involved. Look at your last lesson. What percentage of the time was occupied by teacher talk compared to student talk? When half of the students' talk relates to the lesson, students naturally become engaged in it. It's like the metaphor of the empty vessel versus the flexing muscle. Some teachers approach the student brain as if it were an empty vessel simply waiting for knowledge to be poured in. These teachers focus on input: lectures, videos, readings, and charts. Other teachers approach the student brain as if it were a muscle, believing the only way to strengthen a muscle is to put it to work. These teachers focus on student participation: labs, debates, small groups, and research reports.

I prefer the muscle metaphor. Again, it's a matter of balance. When a teacher asks a question and calls on a conveniently raised hand, one student is engaged while the others are expected to sit and listen. In a typical classroom, those who need the least help tend to get called on (engaged) the most, while those who need the most help tend to spend more time sitting and listening (unengaged). It's the reason tutors have so few classroom management problems. You might well think to yourself, as I did when I started teaching, "If only there were a way to somehow allow all students to answer every question, I'm sure their level of interest would improve."

There is. In fact, there are a variety of ways in which you can have several students answering your questions and contributing ideas at the same time, without creating chaos. Instead of eliciting a single response and moving on during your next lesson, try some of the following techniques.

Essential Methods for Increasing Student Participation

- Choral Responses

- Rapid Individual Turns

- Quiet Group Responses

- Written Group Responses

- Random Turns for Individuals

- Small-Group Short Responses

- Small-Group Long Responses

- Partner Responses

Choral Responses. Given a signal from the teacher, everyone responds in unison. The following is an example of a ten-second sequence of rapid-fire questions and answers:

TEACHER: "OK, let's review. Everyone, what is the job of a plant's chlorophyll? *(Snap fingers.)*

STUDENTS: "To make food."

TEACHER: "That's right, to make food. What color is chlorophyll?" *(Snap fingers.)*

STUDENTS: "Green."

TEACHER: "Good. Where is chlorophyll found in the cell?" *(Snap fingers.)*

STUDENTS: "In the chloroplast."

TEACHER: "Good job. Let's try that sequence again, but a little faster this time."

Rapid Individual Turns. After everyone has responded chorally, quickly check to see if individuals were listening by asking them the same question. It takes only two or three repeats, but it ensures that everyone is attending because they don't know if they will be the next one called. Bonus benefit: because they hear the concept repeated two or three times by other students, they are more likely to remember it. "Lindsay, what's the job of a plant's chlorophyll? Amber, what does chlorophyll do? Keith, why have chlorophyll in a plant?" "Good, the job of green chlorophyll is to make food." Similarly, during oral reading have student readers change every three to five sentences.

Quiet Group Responses. Given a question from the teacher, ask everyone to answer it together without talking. Here is an example:

▶ (Teacher direction) "Whisper to your neighbor what you think the correct answer is."

   (Teacher question) "How many of you heard the right answer from your neighbor?"

▶ "Write in the air your answer to the question."

▶ "Show with the number of fingers you hold high in the air your answer to this problem."

Written Group Responses. Give students a personal chalkboard or 12" x 18" piece of whiteboard. Have them write down their answer and turn it upside down on their desk. Give them a signal, at which point everyone holds up their answer at the same time. Quickly scan the raised boards and either clarify the concept or move on to the next question. (This could also be done on a sheet of paper, but the whiteboard is more cool. "Write on your paper . . . turn it over . . . now show me your answer.")

Random Turns for Individuals. Write student names on popsicle sticks or small cards, one name per stick or card. During a lecture or discussion, use the cup of sticks or deck of cards to select the next person to call on for a response. This does two things. It removes any question of fairness as to who gets the toughest questions to answer. It also ensures that everyone gets to participate. The fact that names are drawn at random keeps everyone listening to every question. When the name of a special-needs student comes up, be aware that you may need to adjust the question.

(Note: Be sure to reshuffle the deck periodically or place the sticks back in the can after a name is read to keep students engaged. Otherwise students already called on may feel that they can just kick back until everyone's name has been called.)

Small-Group Short Responses.

TEACHER: "In your table groups, think of three causes of the Revolutionary War. I will give you four minutes to make your list."

(When the time comes for sharing . . .) "Table 2, what is one of the causes that you thought of?"

(Teacher lists on board.) "Table 5, what did your group come up with?"

(Teacher continues the list and places check marks next to duplicates. This continues until all tables have responded.)

VARIATION: Each student is assigned a number in their group (1–5). Teacher randomly pulls out a number (say, 3), and all 3s must report for their group. This variation ensures that everyone is participating with their group.

Small-Group Long Responses.

TEACHER: "In your table groups and acting as a jury, come up with a verdict for the video case you just watched. Prepare to present your verdict to the class and be prepared to defend the reasons for your decision. If your verdict is not unanimous, explain why you were not able to reach agreement. You will be given 20 minutes to make your decision and another five minutes to prepare your presentation. I will give you two-minute warnings for each deadline."

Partner Responses (aka "pair share," dyads, triads).

For a quick way to give everyone a chance to participate within a minimum amount of time, simply have them share a response with the person sitting next to them. "Why do you think so much of Mark Twain's most popular work was centered around the Mississippi River? I'll give you 45 seconds to think of an answer, then I want you to share your thoughts with the person sitting next to you."

STRATEGY 13 ▶ Keep Your Pacing Crisp And Your Students Active

"With no novelty, there is monotony and boredom. With no routines, there is chaos and anxiety."

(Kagan, 1994)

The attention span of young people is becoming shorter all the time. Researchers tell us that TV, video games, and fast-paced lifestyles are shrinking our ability to attend to a task. Consider these reported findings:

• The attention span of young children is reported to vary by age, from three to five minutes per year of age up to the second grade (Schmitt, 1999).

• A student's attention span is one-half of his or her age (Fortin, 2008).

• The average attention span of a 13-year-old 35 years ago was 15 minutes. Today, the attention span of an average adult is 20 (Reynolds, 2008).

• The attention span of adults in England has fallen from 12 minutes to slightly more than five minutes over the past ten years (*Thaindian News*, Lloyd's TSB Report, 2008).

Essentials for Keeping Pacing Crisp and Students Active

- Pick up the pace.

- Move beyond the rote.

- Break up the boredom, change the pace.

- Use "sponge activities."

When we exceed our students' ability to attend to a single task, problems with their behavior are inevitable. You need to be aware that today's students are conditioned to fast-paced interaction through their video games and action-oriented media, and you need to respond to it. Changing from one task to another when their attention span has maxed out is as much a strategy for behavior management as for instruction.

We actually encourage behavior problems when our pacing slows. By nature, we tend to overreact to misbehavior, then and there, right in front of the entire class. When we do, though, we interrupt the lesson and slow the pace. Some teachers will hold up the entire class for prolonged periods until a single student stops his or her disruption, then do it again when another student acts up. Some teachers intentionally conduct their lessons slowly and carefully so they can better monitor the behavior of the class. Some accept all student questions and anecdotes, believing them to be an indication of the interest of the entire class. These approaches may make intuitive sense, but they actually work against us.

The behavior of our students can be a barometer of our instruction. When we listen to that barometer and respond by making instructional adjustments, we can prevent many of the behavior problems we would otherwise have to confront.

Research on the brain has taught us that students need a predictable pattern in classroom routines in order for them to feel comfortable and less anxious. On the other hand, novelty makes us more alert and attentive, and it evokes emotions that help us better remember the content of our lessons (Kagan, 1994). This presents a dilemma: how can we provide both predictability *and* novelty? The solution to this dilemma is to provide a balance between novelty and routine.

REFLECTION QUESTION

What does my students' behavior signal about my instruction?

Pick up the pace. Student misbehavior can be an important signal for us if we will hear it. The signal is to step up the pacing of the lesson. Moving quickly through your directions, lecture, or class discussion actually builds interest and, along with it, student attention. Most of the class will keep up just fine. If a few are not able to, you can catch them up later or ask an assigned peer "buddy" to repeat the directions during independent practice. The key point here is to keep the interest of the class high by keeping the pacing brisk. To help you ensure rapid pacing, try some of these strategies:

• Plan in advance the key points you want students to take away from your directions or lecture, then write them down. Move through your list quickly, using it to help you stay on track and covering all major points within the time allocated. If you have more time remaining, have the students review using some of the methods described in Strategy 12.

• Accept only three or four questions before moving forward, to keep general interest high. (You might let them know that you will be able to take other questions or comments at a later time.)

- Write an outline of your major points on the whiteboard. Use this as the framework for your discussion, referring to it often. Both you and your students can see how much must be covered in the time remaining. (Middle school students might also use this outline to begin learning the skill of note taking.)

- Employ a rhythm when having students chorally recite a list or spell a word. Use finger snaps to keep that rhythm fast. For example, "Everyone, what are the six basic food groups?" *(snap . . . snap . . . snap . . . snap . . . snap . . . snap)* "One more time, a little faster though."

- Make an audio recording of a presentation, then listen to yourself later. Note where students may have sidetracked you from your main points with too many questions or comments, or you paused too long to process a disruption. Note also if you are keeping your own interest level high.

Move beyond the rote. Invite students to explore their own thoughts and perceptions. Instead of requiring the quickest students to wait for the rest of the class, periodically set them free to address the subject in a creative way of their own choosing.

▶ Pose questions that begin with the words "Predict . . .," "Imagine . . .," "Compare . . .," "Contrast . . .," and "Evaluate . . .,"

▶ "How might you . . .?"

▶ "What problems might arise if . . .?"

▶ "What are some of the strengths of . . .?"

▶ "What is your opinion about that decision?"

▶ "What would happen if . . .?"

▶ "Explain how you arrived at that answer."

Break up the boredom with a change of pace. Even though the daily routine prescribes work on a self-starter activity, change it up a little with an unusual and novel topic or task. ("List three shows you wish you could see on TV this season." "Draw a book cover for the novel you are reading." "Complete this word puzzle.") Surprise them with something unexpected, a little out of the ordinary.

• Post a riddle of the day, cartoon, comic strip, or a funny quote. Call attention to it when you feel the lesson beginning to drag.

• Give them an unusual way to signal you in the course of a class discussion. "Stand on your chair when you have finished this step." (I picked this up from a junior high teacher teaching a keyboarding class.)

• Switch frequently between writing, creating a map, drawing a picture, solving a problem, interacting with a partner, developing a category system, acting, singing, speculating, etc.

• Schedule a monthly, 30-minute special activity (crazy hat day, favorite music day, pizza party, stand-up comic day, Shakespearean English day, etc.).

• Plan a walking field trip to catalogue community services within a quarter mile of the school (sewer, power, water, police, fire, transportation, zoning regulations, etc.).

Web sites containing lists of elementary and middle school sponge activities:

▲ http://www.educationworld.com/a_lesson/lesson168.shtml

▲ http://www.everydayteaching.com/Helpers/sponge.html

▲ http://faculty.mwsu.edu/west/maryann.coe/coe/sponge.htm

▲ http://coe.sdsu.edu/people/jmora/MoraModules/vocabularydev.htm

▲ http://content.scholastic.com/browse/article.jsp?id=3745695

Use sponge activities. Sometimes lessons move more quickly than we planned, or a critical teaching aid is unexpectedly unavailable. When we stretch a lesson out to fill up a little remaining time, it usually gets run into the ground. Madeline Hunter (2004, p. 29) suggested that we keep a collection of "sponge" activities on hand to turn those few minutes of time into another productive learning opportunity. A few examples are listed here, along with Web sites that contain many more.

• Tell a progressive story in which one student tells three sentences and then passes to the next student, the next, and the next.

• Turn to your neighbor. One of you tell the other about an interesting experience you have had. The listener must be prepared to retell the story to the class.

• Write: (a) an abbreviation, (b) a Roman numeral, (c) a trademark, (d) a proper name (biographical), (e) a proper name (geographical).

- Write a list of . . .

  —things that are white and fluffy

  —things that you do on a Saturday

  —things a pioneer might eat

  —different kinds of transportation

  —chemicals you would find in your house

  —kinds of bodywork a car might need

  —an animal for each letter of the alphabet

  —ways to protect your identity

- Have each student pick one important event in history and write it down, then line up in a time line tracing the order of these events.

- Design a travel brochure for the perfect vacation. How will people get there? Where will it be? What can people do there? How long will it last? Share three or four with the class.

STRATEGY 14 ▶ Plan Lessons With Crafty Care

Sometimes there are a few critical rough patches in the course of a lesson that snowball into bigger problems as the class period goes on. When you notice a recurring pattern of these events, that is your signal to develop a plan to smooth them out in advance. By addressing them up front you will save yourself and your class unnecessary frustration, aggravation, and confrontation. Teachers who plan for these rough spots have classes that are far more orderly, controlled, and productive. Over time, teachers begin to develop a sense of the dramatic in their lesson planning. They gradually pick up a few tricks and tactics that can generate high student interest, even if the content does not hold any inherent fascination. They anticipate problems and have alternatives in their hip pocket that they pull out at the first sign of trouble. By being a little crafty in their planning and inserting these tactics at strategic points in their lesson, these teachers can maintain student interest for hours. As you gain more experience and further develop your own style of teaching, you will instinctively smooth out these rough spots in your plans. To get you started, we describe six planning tactics to address these critical rough spots.

REFLECTION QUESTIONS

How will I ensure that I am not expecting students to sit quietly with nothing to do? In what ways will students actively participate in the lesson?

What will early completers do while they are waiting for the others?

What will I do to motivate students to succeed?

Stop while it's still interesting. This could be a caveat for every great lesson. A common mistake that teachers make is to allow a successful activity to run too long. Students get engaged, interest is high, everyone is on task, and we are feeling great. It's going so well, let's enjoy the moment a little longer . . . .

Wrong! It is specifically because an activity is so successful that we want to stop it while student interest is still high. Despite the groans and pleas to keep going, stop the activity and transition on to the next section of your lesson plan. To stop is to keep the activity alive for future use. The tactic here is to use the memory of this successful activity to keep the motivation high the next time you use it. If you run their interest into the ground, it will be much more difficult to tap into that interest again. Stopping while it's still engaging preserves that interest level. You will almost guarantee that interest will be just as high next week or the week after when you try it again. Over the course of the year, you will have garnered much more on-task behavior with your great teaching strategy than the few extra minutes you enjoyed the day you ran the activity until they tired of it.

Planning Strategies for Preventing Behavior Problems

- Stop while it's still interesting.

- Plan for a sequence of success.

- Know the answer to this question: what will they *do*?

- Plan for preferred modalities.

- Use student ideas.

- Stay on the move.

Sequence of success. Success inspires success. Nothing gives more confidence to try something new than experiencing success in a previous attempt. Children who do not think they can succeed will often misbehave rather than show their peers that they don't understand. This is their smoke screen to hide failure or a fear of failure.

Sequence your instruction in small enough increments that students (especially those at risk) can feel successful. The more widely used commercial curricula are designed to do just this. Be sure that your units incorporate frequent opportunities for them to demonstrate success. Take care, also, to notice that success, then to publicly acknowledge and praise it.

When a student is stuck and needs a little extra help, use a Praise-Prompt-Check-Recheck sequence. Start with a statement that acknowledges the work (or behavior) that he or she has done well to this point. Provide the needed prompt so that he or she can move to the next level (one step at a time, keep it short and simple, be very specific). Check for understanding by having the student repeat the procedure. Then check back with praise for the successful work the student completes independently.

Praise-Prompt-Check-Recheck

Example for Grades 3–5:

▶ "Mike, I see that you were able to get the first two problems correct." (Praise)

▶ "Remember to carry that remainder like we did together on the board." (Prompt)

▶ "Let me watch you do that problem again. Good job. I think you've got it." (Check)

▶ (Leave and return again) "Now how did you do with the fourth problem? Super job!" (Recheck)

Example for Grades 6 and Up:

▶ "Kimie, you were smart to look up the different classes of animals as a way to identify this one." (Praise)

▶ "Now take another look to see if you have considered all of the classes. Let's take out that list of animal classes." (Prompt)

▶ "Is there a class or two that you did not actually rule out? OK, what are the characteristics of those classes? Now you're on the right track." (Check)

▶ (Leave and return again) "What animal did it turn out to be? Excellent!" (Recheck)

What will they *do*? Plan with this question in mind. Minimize the amount of time during which the answer would be, "sit and listen." The more time they are expected to sit and listen, the greater the risk of problems with classroom behavior. This is especially important for early completers who cannot (and should not be expected to) wait quietly for the others to catch up.

In the list of teaching methods below, types of instruction are listed in the order that some researchers say that students are able to retain the information taught over a 24-hour period of time, from the greatest retention to the least (Cohen, Manion, and Morrison, 2004, p. 175). Consider how you might rank this list in the order of frequency that they are used in most classrooms. The contrast is frightening.

1. Teaching others   90%

2. Practice by doing   75%

3. Discussion groups	50%
4. Demonstration	30%
5. Audio-visual	20%
6. Reading	10%
7. Lecture	5%

While the validity of these numbers has been questioned, it has been clearly demonstrated that "multi-modal learning" can increase learning retention by up to 32 percentile points. "The reality is that the most effective designs for learning adapt to include a variety of media, combinations of modalities, levels of interactivity, learner characteristics, and pedagogy based on a complex set of circumstances" (Fadel and Lemke, 2008, p. 14).

The answer to the question, "What will they do?" is to get them actively participating, using a variety of experiences, activities, interactions, and physical tasks. Try some of these ideas:

• Share with a partner.

• Participate chorally with others and through individual turns.

• Fill in a lecture outline.

• Teach your dyad or triad what you learned about . . .

• Design a display.

• Circle all of the letters *w* and *m* you can find in this newspaper clipping.

• Complete a worksheet.

• Conduct and explain this experiment for your group.

• List three reasons for . . .

• Prepare arguments for a debate.

- Construct a map or graph.

- Find key concepts in a textbook chapter.

- Color and cut out a paper figure.

Preferred modalities. Clearly not all of us learn in the same way. Some of us are more comfortable in a verbal mode, others in a visual mode, and still others in a physical mode. While it would not be reasonable to expect teachers to teach in each individual's preferred learning style and background, it is reasonable for these three major modalities to be included in each unit of instruction.

Teachers are most proficient in the verbal modality. We talk and discuss, explain and expound, articulate and clarify, direct and correct. All of this seems to work for most, but it can leave others confused and frustrated. The students who don't "get it" after a verbal presentation are the ones most likely to cause problems later.

Enrich your lesson by incorporating the other two modalities as well. In the visual modality, try summary graphics, pictures, visual prompts, posted lecture outlines, mind maps, story webs, time lines, flow charts, pie graphs, and sequence cycles. In the physical modality, try project models and displays, structured movement in the room, learning centers, dramatic enactments, math manipulatives, student chalkboard presentations, and small-group reports. A Chinese proverb reminds us about the importance of modalities:

I hear . . . I forget.

I see . . . I remember.

I do . . . I understand.

Use student ideas. Student interest builds when they hear from other students. They become full participants in the learning process, and thus fully engaged in their own learning. We see the same effect in our own learning style. Whenever we make a presentation, draw conclusions, generate new ideas, and explore conflicting points of view, we become fully engaged in the topic. The minds of children are not empty vessels waiting to be filled with knowledge from on high. They are active muscles that develop only when they are exercised. The good news for teachers is this: it is in their nature to yearn for exercise! When you plan your lessons, include an opportunity for students to develop and share their own ideas and conclusions. For example:

- Have six students go to the whiteboard, write the steps of a math problem from their seatwork assignment, then take turns explaining their work to the class.

- Have each table group brainstorm the implications of the scientific principle just explained, then report their ideas to the rest of the class.

- Have students prepare a two-minute oral report on a book they have read. Provide the structure of the content of that report and have them rehearse it with a partner in advance to check for time. Use two or three of these reports for a sponge activity or to help settle the class after lunch or recess.

Stay on the move. Your proximity alone builds student interest and attention. It is also a crafty tool to enhance your more traditional teaching methods. Consider the following:

SEATWORK. Your changing proximity enables you to check for understanding when you monitor their work as you move around the class. Here is a timely opportunity to provide personal clarifications, correct a misunderstanding, and reward good work with a positive comment. You know what is going on in your class because you are there to see it firsthand at the level of the individual student.

LECTURE. Teacher movement is a wonderful enhancement of a lecture. Professional entertainers, politicians, and keynote speakers use this skill all of the time. Their constant movement both on the stage and into the audience helps them to hold the attention of the crowd, without which they would be out of a job. The heads of the audience are constantly moving with them. Not only does all this movement add interest, it helps the audience to better connect with the speaker. The listeners see the speaker from different angles, hear from different perspectives of sound, and perk right up when the attention of the audience is directed to someone standing close to where they are sitting. So it is with a teacher who is lecturing in a classroom of students.

DISCUSSION. Classroom discussions are much more fluid. The ebb and flow of attention is often unpredictable, making it even more interesting. But some students "check out" in a discussion. They are happy to allow four or five others to carry the discussion and create the illusion in the teacher's mind that everyone is fully involved. Teachers who walk around the room during a discussion are much more aware of who is and who is not participating. Their physical presence enables them to see more clearly who needs encouragement, who needs to expand on an incomplete thought, and who needs to let others participate as well. Their presence also brings the spotlight of class attention to every corner of the room.

INDEPENDENT GROUP WORK. Small groups are a powerful instructional tool for keeping students engaged in their learning, but they need careful monitoring in order to be effective. It is too easy for small groups to get sidetracked and find themselves off task. Teacher proximity serves three purposes in small-group activities: 1) it provides an early warning if a group is straying off task,

2) it gives the group an opportunity to seek clarification when the teacher is conveniently walking by, and 3) it helps the teacher to check for student understanding of the core concepts to be learned. Even when working directly with one small group, you must use eye contact as you talk with them, then continue to circulate throughout the room.

TEACHER-DIRECTED GROUP WORK. Proximity control is crucial with teacher-led small groups as well. You need to be aware not only of how students are performing in the small group sitting in front of you, but you must also be scanning the behavior of the rest of the class. Seat your small group within arms' reach and where soft voices can be heard. Seat yourself so that you can easily scan the rest of the class while still directing your small group. At least as often as small groups change, get out of your seat and walk around the class. If on-task behavior is beginning to suffer, give your small group an independent task and circulate through the class more often.

CHAPTER 5

Interventions:

WHEN THEY MISBEHAVE, *DO* SOMETHING

• • •

When a student disrupts your class, you need to intervene so that the disruption does not stop you from teaching or your students from learning. If we fail to act, we tacitly condone the disruption. Marzano's meta-analysis of 68 studies on classroom management showed that there is a decrease in classroom disruptions of 32 percentile points when teachers effectively used interventions in their classrooms. This held true across all grade levels: a 25 point decrease at the high school level, 28 points in middle schools, 33 points in upper elementary, and 35 points in the primary grades (Marzano, 2003).

So what would it take to change that student's behavior? It depends on the student and the circumstances. Fortunately, you have a rich array of options available to you. How do you decide which to use? As explained in Chapter 1, there are two considerations as you make this decision:

1. Is it the least intrusive correction necessary to do the job?

2. Does it preserve the dignity of the student?

The more benevolent of the interventions available are founded on the assumption that less is more. The least intrusive interventions take much less energy for you and, because they do not call the class's attention to the problem, preserve student dignity. They allow teaching and learning to continue by preventing a minor infraction from becoming a major disruption. As long as they correct the behavior, they are sufficient. If simply standing next to a student changes his behavior, nothing further is needed. You have corrected the behavior without allowing it to get blown out of proportion.

Consider this common situation: you are sitting in the back of the room working with a small group of students. Two students who should be doing seatwork begin talking quietly with each other. You look up, notice what they are doing, and simply say their names. Now there are pretty good odds that this will be enough to get them back on task. Again, you have accomplished the needed correction without a confrontation or even a formal consequence.

Be patient. Nothing works every time or in every circumstance. If one doesn't work this time, simply select another intervention for the next time. Fortunately, this chapter describes many powerful interventions from which you can choose!

STRATEGY 15 ▶ The Clipboard Technique

Students need to know that their behavior is noticed and that it makes a difference. A clipboard is one effective way of communicating this. This is particularly useful for middle school and older elementary students. The strategy is simple and easy to use. The teacher carries a clipboard during class. When a student misbehaves, the teacher moves closer to the student and, in an obvious manner, places a mark on the clipboard. Similarly, when the teacher uses a social cue to notice students who are on task, the teacher again places a mark on the clipboard.

So what are these marks good for? This data could be used in a private conference with a student who is working on improving his behavior. It could be used for a class-wide incentive of bonus time for a special activity or an assignment cut in half. It could be used to monitor individual behavior contracts, give parents feedback on their child's progress, or support a referral for special services to the school's multidisciplinary team. It could also be used in a call to parents to discuss a problem or commend a child on an especially good day. The rewards and consequences that you select are actually less important than the fact that your students know that you are noticing and keeping track of their behavior.

That is the real power of this strategy. When the student notices the teacher making a mark on that clipboard, he knows that the teacher means business. That mark communicates that the student is not invisible. His or her behavior is noticed and is now a matter of record, for good or for bad. Now that it is in writing, he or she can be held accountable for any misbehavior. The strategy is made even more powerful when it is paired with teacher proximity (Strategy 4) and social cues (Strategy 1).

REFLECTION QUESTIONS

Do students know I am keeping track of their behavior?

Are they held accountable?

This strategy also preserves the dignity of the student. Because he or she is not singled out in front of the class, there is no need to become defensive or to bluster in anger to save face in front of his or her peers. Because accountability and consequences are applied in private when time allows, emotion does not enter in to undermine our relationships. Because the marks provide you with explicit data, corrections can be based on that data instead of misperceptions (including the perception that "the teacher doesn't like me").

Essential Components of the Clipboard Technique

- Carry the class roster with you.

- Show you notice.

- Use the data.

- Notice the positive and use incentives.

Notice also how easy this strategy is for the teacher to use. When the teacher picks up the clipboard, students know that their behavior is about to be explicitly monitored. It is not necessary for the teacher to constantly carry a clipboard. It is when the class is getting restless, during risky transitions, or during times when you feel the need for a little extra control that you use the clipboard strategy. It is not necessary to mark every student every day. You are gathering explicit data on students whose behavior needs correction, and using the clipboard to give credit in the form of a social cue to students who are meeting your expectations.

As you become more sophisticated in using this strategy, you will be able to make another important use of the positive points. Some students who are often in trouble for their behavior believe themselves to be troublemakers. It becomes part of their identity. The positive marks that record when the student is "caught being good" can also be used to foster a new and different identity while in your class.

Class roster. Make several copies of your class roster, with horizontal lines for each student. Divide the page into vertical columns. Two columns can be used for marking either desired behavior (positive comments) or misbehavior (breaking the class rules). Additional vertical columns could be used to categorize marks by rule, days of the week, or periods of the day. Try different formats to see what works best for you.

Show you notice. Carry your clipboard as you walk through the room monitoring student behavior. When a student misbehaves, take a few steps toward the student and make eye contact. Place a mark next to the student's name on the clipboard. Then move on. As long as the student notices you making that mark, there is no need to say anything at this point.

Use the data. When your marks show that a student is showing a pattern of misbehavior, address it in a private conference with the student later (e.g., after class, after school, during quiet seatwork, back at your desk, during a preparation period). Use the marks as the basis for a discussion about the student's behavior.

Notice the positive and use incentives. It is important that you notice good behavior as well. Periodically give a social cue or other positive comment for desired behaviors, then make a mark next to the named students. You may also want to establish some class-wide incentives for an accumulation of positive marks. This will contribute to the positive nature of your classroom climate.

Target Behavior

Teaching the class rules does not necessarily mean that our behavior problems are over. Concerns about specific behaviors or behaviors during particular transitions will continue to crop up throughout the school year. Here are two common scenarios new teachers encounter:

> *Miss Morison's fourth grade class is well into the daily routines, now that it is early October. It does bother her, however, when her students take far too much time to move into their centers during reading. She has gone over the class rules several times, but they still dally and talk during this particular transition.*

> *Mr. Haltiner's eighth grade math classes can't seem to enter class without talking, laughing, and general horseplay. It's as if hall behavior enters the classroom with them. It takes far too long for the classes to settle down to task, even though he has reviewed the class rules many times over the three weeks since school began.*

These concerns must be faced head-on, and the sooner they are addressed the better. However, it is not necessary to review every rule in order to address a particular behavior. Instead, designate that concern as a "target behavior" to narrow your focus.

Start by taking a minute to think it through. What exactly is the behavior that is concerning you? That is your target behavior. What should it look like and sound like instead? That is your expectation. How will you communicate this to the students? That is your intervention. Here is how it works:

Convene a class meeting. Schedule a short class meeting to share your concern with your students. Level with them. Describe the behavior you are concerned about as precisely as possible and why it is concerning to you. Tell them when or under what circumstances it is occurring, what it is looking and sounding like, and what concerns you about it. Then describe how you expect their behavior to look like and sound like instead.

Rehearse. In some situations you will want to take the time to rehearse the behavior. Miss Morison might have her class quickly walk through the transition of moving to their centers the right way, then immediately return to their seats to finish the class meeting. Mr. Haltiner's students may need to go back into the hallway and re-enter the class the right way. He might also decide that instead of rehearsing how they should enter the class, he will give them instructions that are absolutely precise, specific, and clear, then walk through it himself as a demonstration. In either case, the students see a very concrete example of what meeting his expectations looks like.

Monitor. After you have taught the new behavior, the next step is crucial. These two teachers in the examples (page 92) must now monitor that behavior. This is the key step that tells the students that the teacher is serious about this expectation.

How to Focus on a Single Target Behavior

- Convene a class meeting.

- Rehearse the desired behavior.

- Monitor the target behavior.

- Convene a follow-up class meeting.

- Periodically review that target behavior.

Elementary Reading Centers:

"OK, it's now time to move to our reading centers. Let's review what that should look like." The teacher solicits student descriptions. "Today I am going to be watching very carefully to see who remembers to move to their center the right way. When I say go, you can begin moving."

▶ "Marcus and Juan are walking quietly. Thank you."

▶ "Thanks to Adam and Victoria who are walking without touching anyone."

▶ "James, you will need to return to your desk and start again."

▶ "Jake, Melissa, and Anthony remembered to keep their hands to themselves. Good job."

▶ "Emma, Juliana, and Sophie have started their work right away."

Middle School Math Class:

"Tomorrow I am going to be watching carefully to see if you can enter the class and begin your self-starter the right way."

Tomorrow comes, and Mr. Haltiner must be ready. The self-starter is in place. He positions himself so that he has an uninterrupted view of the door, and the students will have a clear view of him. The bell rings. As the students enter and begin the transition, he uses social cues to remind them about his expectations.

▶ "Thanks for entering quietly, Nolan."

▶ "Carmen, Bella, Luis, nice job of coming into the room quietly today."

▶ "Ari and Sylvan remembered how to enter the room today. Thank you."

▶ "I can see that as you get seated you are now getting right to work. That is so helpful."

▶ "Troy and John, you need to go back into the hall and try entering again. OK, much better. Thank you."

▶ "Thanks to Robert, Chad, Shane, and Connie for getting right to work."

Follow-up class meeting. Once the event is completed and the class has reassembled (in these examples, that would be after the self-starter or after the reading centers), it is time for a brief follow-up class meeting. The teacher reviews how the class handled the situation that had been creating the problem behaviors, offering praise and thanks for success. The teacher reviews rough spots and gives cautions as well.

Periodic review. It is prudent to periodically review your target behavior, by calling the attention of the class to the expected behavior, announcing that today or tomorrow you will again be looking specifically for this target behavior, and using social cues to reinforce and maintain success. If the behavior is not meeting your expectations, it is entirely appropriate to go through this sequence again.

For some classes, one intervention is enough. For others, it may take a few repetitions to strengthen the desired behavior. You may need to monitor that target behavior for several days for it to become firm.

Use the target behavior strategy *before* you get so frustrated with the class that you lose your cool. It communicates your needs without punishment or anger. It corrects a behavior problem without diminishing anyone's dignity. It emphasizes and even highlights student success and self-confidence. Finally, the very fact that you are explicitly monitoring behavior and holding students accountable has a positive spin-off effect on other classroom behaviors.

REFLECTION QUESTION

If I could select one behavior to change in my class, what would it be?

STRATEGY 17 ▶ **"In the Moment" Interventions**

Not every misbehavior has to result in a huge confrontation. Overreactions tend to create a negative classroom climate and a perception that class behavior is worse than it really is. Teachers who overcorrect tend to wear themselves out very quickly. They also tend to get angry faster and more often than their colleagues.

Sometimes all it takes is a simple reminder to bring the student quickly back on task. Most children want to comply with teacher expectations. This is true in both elementary and secondary classrooms. Because they are children, they often forget where the lines are or misidentify their behavior as barely acceptable when it really is not. When this is the case, a simple reminder will do.

Because we assume benevolence, and because we want to use the least intrusive corrections to achieve acceptable behavior, we give a subtle reminder. We give that reminder "in the moment" so that any delay in responding is not interpreted by the rest of the class as an endorsement of that behavior. The method we use in giving that reminder is important. By giving it when the behavior occurs we must not disrupt the work of other students in the class or the instruction we are delivering.

"The Look." Some teachers have developed a facial expression that can communicate volumes without a single word. A pause, eye contact, and a raised eyebrow can tell a student to settle down faster than any verbal directive, and do so without interrupting teaching and learning. You have probably seen or experienced this yourself. Try it out in front of a mirror or your spouse, then test it out for yourself. A caution: use it with restraint. Overuse will weaken the effect and may cause early onset facial wrinkles.

> ## Interventions That Provide an Essential Reminder in the Moment
>
> - "The Look"
>
> - "The Voice"
>
> - "The Presence"

"The Voice." Your tone of voice can reveal a lot about your confidence level and how serious you are about your expectations. You want to speak in a firm voice, not a tentative one. You want to speak with the self-assurance and confidence that communicates 1) you are in charge, 2) you know what you are doing, and 3) you know how to respond if they do not follow your directions. This is not a voice that is asking. It is a voice that is telling, with authority. It is not a mean or hostile voice, but an assertive voice with a level but direct character. "Shayla, I need you to stop doing that. Thank you." Tape record yourself and listen for the authority in your voice. Listen and compare voices in your daily life. Compare the professional voices of police, construction workers, and football coaches with the voices of retail salespeople, waiters, and hotel concierges. I can think of no better illustration of voice.

Another strategy is to whisper in your own class during quiet seatwork. If you want students to be quietly completing their seatwork, model for them the quiet behavior you are seeking. Whisper answers to questions. Whisper clarifications as you move around the room gauging students' understanding. Whisper directives or corrections to individuals. The climate of this independent work time is like a library in which everyone, including the teacher, is respecting individual concentration by whispering.

"The Presence." Your presence itself can be an intervention. Strategy 4 describes teacher proximity as a preventative tool. Proximity is also an intervention tool to block an emerging disruption. If you've given "the look" and a change did not occur, smile and walk slowly toward the student. Standing next to a student who is talking in class can have an immediate effect, again, without speaking a single word or using a single minute of class time. If your district allows this, a touch on the shoulder is an effective intervention for some students. Students talking to each other will stop simply because the teacher is approaching. Teacher proximity is a tool you do not want to be without.

STRATEGY 18 ▶ Directed Response Interventions

There are certainly times when the more subtle interventions are not working as well as you might have hoped. You tried them, but for whatever reason you did not get the student's attention, or the student was too distracted to read the signals you were sending. You now need to respond directly to the student so that your message will not go unnoticed or be misunderstood. These four tactics will take your intervention to the next level.

Changing location. Changing a student's location can be remarkably effective. Some students should simply not sit together. Some need a little time away from a stressful situation. Others need a new perspective just to change their mind-set before their behavior escalates to the point of disruption. Your arsenal of interventions should include a change of seating.

Interventions That Provide a Directed Response

- Changing Location ("Seat Away")
- "Assumption of Compliance"
- "Negative Assertion" and "Passive Confrontation"
- Forced Choice

A NEW PERSPECTIVE: Anna is fidgety today. She just can't seem to settle down to her work and her whispering seems to be pulling her neighbors off task as well. You have given her "the eye" and used your proximity, but it is only a short while before she is back at it. You smile, calmly walk to her desk, bend down, and whisper, "Would you mind sitting over here for a while?" You assume compliance and slowly walk away. Because your approach is not confrontational and kept private between the two of you, she is far more likely to comply. To give her a little time and distance to comply on her own, simply walk away. (She may now be thinking, "I'll move when I say it's time to move.") If she has not moved after a few minutes, return to her desk and give her a choice: "I notice you haven't moved. You can certainly talk to me about it after school instead. I'll let you choose." Then you smile and calmly walk away.

SEAT AWAY: Ryan is in a bad mood today. He starts an argument with Jacob, and some anger begins to show. You smile, calmly walk over to Ryan, point to an empty desk in the back of the class (see Strategy 6), and quietly say, "Ryan, I need you to take a seat away for a little while." This is a cooling-off time for Ryan. He is not banished for the rest of the period, day, or week. He is simply given a time to settle and refocus. When it is convenient for you (and the heat of the moment has passed), slowly walk over to the seat away, bend down, and quietly invite him to tell you what's happening. (See also Strategy 19.) Restate your need for a quiet class in order to teach, then tell him he can return to his desk as soon as he thinks he is ready (Rhode, Jenson, and Reavis, 1994).

Assumption of Compliance. A teacher who gives a directive and then stares at the student until he or she complies runs the risk of creating a disruption in front of the entire class. The student feels backed into a corner. Our tough-to-teach students will argue, accelerate the confrontation, or comply with a visible display of resentment. In any case, this disrupts instruction and damages our relationship.

Jim Fay (1995, p. 323) suggests that after directing or correcting a student, we should assume compliance. Simply give the direction in private, say "thank you," break eye contact, and then step away to continue your instruction, giving the student the time and space to make a decision about what to do next.

> Example: David is not doing his independent work. He shows much more interest in getting Jolene's attention. You calmly approach David, bend down, and whisper, "Would you mind getting back to your work? Thanks." You don't wait for an answer. Instead you smile, turn your back, and slowly move away from him. You assume David's compliance and continue with your instruction or monitoring.

The teacher has chosen to intervene by giving David a simple directive delivered with a calm and smiling assumption of compliance. This technique gives David respect, dignity, privacy, and the teacher's trust that he will comply with the directive. As an added benefit, the method could actually strengthen the teacher's relationship with David because the quiet voice preserved his dignity and conveyed respect. This intervention is easy for the teacher and often sufficient to its purpose.

"Negative Assertion" and "Passive Confrontation."

Here's an interesting game: it's called "last word." Whoever gets in the last word wins. The student leads. The teacher responds. The student retorts in turn. The teacher responds again and begins to get angry. The student counters, and so does the teacher, but even angrier this time. And so it goes, until the class is fully entertained and either the teacher or the student blows up in a huge display of anger and defensiveness.

Oops, we just witnessed a power struggle getting blown out of proportion. The surprise outcome: regardless of who actually got the last word, the student won.

Better response: refuse to engage. There are two techniques for avoiding this kind of engagement. The first is what Jim Fay (1995, p. 121) calls the "negative assertion." You smile, agree with the negative the student said (without sarcasm), redirect with a comment or question, then break eye contact and walk away.

Example:

STUDENT: "This class sucks."

TEACHER: "Probably so."

STUDENT: "I hate this work."

TEACHER: "Thanks for sharing that. What are you supposed to be doing now?"

STUDENT: Rolls his eyes and shakes his head.

TEACHER: "Nice try. Now turn your workbook to page 54." Then smile, slowly turn, and walk away.

The second technique is a "passive confrontation." You smile, slowly walk to the student's desk, take two relaxing breaths, keep your mouth closed, and wait. When the student finally gets back to work, smile, say "thank you," then slowly walk away. The student will likely make several attempts to engage you, to which you do not respond. It takes a little time, but your patience, calmness, slow and controlled movements, and refusal to neither tolerate talking back nor engage in it makes a powerful statement.

> "It takes one fool to backtalk. It takes two fools to make a conversation out of it."
>
> (Fred Jones, 2000, p. 225)

Forced choice. When it is time to confront a student directly, teachers certainly prefer compliance to an argument or, worse, defiance. A simple format change in your confrontation can make a huge difference. It is important to remember here that your goal is compliance. Getting the student working on an acceptable task in an acceptable way is your definition of success.

We know that everyone needs some degree of control over his or her life. It could even be considered a basic human need. Personal choice is a foundation of our identity, independence, competence, trustworthiness, and self-worth. It is the measure of the amount of control we possess over our life. This is useful information for those who recognize its value.

When confronting a student, offer a choice. That choice provides the student with a form of control over his or her own destiny. It places the student in a rational frame of mind. It also preserves personal dignity, deflects some of the anger you may be harboring, and it gives the student an honorable escape out of an escalating situation.

The choices you provide must be choices you are comfortable with. If you notice the student is off task, you walk up to the student, bend down, and quietly ask if the student would prefer to do what is assigned or select an alternative activity that is acceptable to you. Since the outcome you desire is compliance, not subjugation, your likelihood of achieving success rises dramatically.

Examples:

- "Feel free to do this assignment with the students at your table or complete it by yourself."

- "Some kids would tell Annette they are sorry this happened, and some would write her a short note of apology. What do you think would be most comfortable for you?"

- "Would you rather cool off here in the classroom or do you think somewhere else would be better?"

- "You need to complete this paper this week. Which deadline would work best for you, Thursday or Friday?"

- "You are welcome to play this game by the rules or watch others play the game so you can learn the rules."

- "You can either work on this assignment now or you can read your library novel and do the assignment at home."

STRATEGY 19 ▶ Private Conference Interventions

Sometimes an incident is so severe that much more process is called for, or you need more time to deal with an incident, or a student has established a pattern of disruption that needs a more direct approach. When the less intrusive interventions described in Strategies 17 and 18 are not effective, it is time for a private conference with the student. This is another place in which the relationship that you have built with your students will be invaluable. Even without a good relationship, the private conference is a powerful strategy.

Because you can't leave your class in the heat of the moment, you need to delay your response. You don't have to resolve everything immediately. Your first priority is instruction. It is perfectly reasonable to hold off your conference until everyone else in the class is working independently. You can defer processing the problem until recess, lunch, after school, or even the next day. A delayed conference will also give you another benefit: time to create distance from the emotions surrounding the problem. This will not only settle the students involved, but it will help to settle you as well. When emotional energy has a chance to defuse, it is easier to approach the situation in a more rational state of mind.

What happens to the student while you delay? Depending on the circumstances, you have several choices. The student might simply continue with the current activity until the time is right, sit in the back of the class (see "seat away" in Strategy 18), wait for you in the hall, or wait for you in the office.

Examples:

- "Lindsay, you and I need to talk at recess."

- "Sheena, that's not appropriate. We will need to talk about this after school."

- "Landon, I can see that you and I need to talk. Would you wait for me out in the hall?"

- "Chris, I need you to wait for me in the office. I will be there to talk with you as soon as I can."

Having pulled the student aside at recess, in the back of the room, or in the hallway, what do you say? Certainly you want to give the student the opportunity to tell his side of the story. Everyone is entitled to fundamental due process. In this kind of conference, your first job is to gather facts, rationally and calmly. I find that taking notes of the major points the student is making has a calming effect on me.

Students are great at tuning out lectures. They are also very practiced in denial and shifting blame to others, so the long and angry lecture probably will not be the most effective intervention for you. If you think about it, showing your temper and losing your calm actually provides the student a great new tool. The student now knows one of your buttons that can be pushed. Beyond the preachy lecture or angry scolding, there are a few structured approaches that produce longer-term benefits.

Four Private Conference Interventions

- The "I Message"

- Call the Parents

- "Reality Therapy"

- "Logical Consequences"

The "I MESSAGE" conference in the hall. When you confront misbehaving students they become defensive. This defensiveness can block our ability to calmly reason with them. It can also cause the student to resist any directives imposed by the teacher. The "I Message" is a tool to relieve some of this defensiveness by reframing the conversation in terms of the teacher's concern with the student's actions. It gives the student information without a directive to act on it, thus avoiding a power struggle (Gordon, 1974).

The classic "I Message" is very simple. It has three parts. It is a non-blameful *description* of the student's behavior, the *effect* that this behavior has on the teacher or the class, and the *feelings* that the teacher has about that effect. It is a method of confronting the student's behavior without attacking the student. In effect, it is a request for the student's help. When presented in this way, the student is more likely to change his or her behavior (Gordon 1974).

- "I don't know if you know it or not, but when you talk back in class that undermines me in front of the class. I feel pretty angry when that happens."

- "When you put down other students, it makes them feel pretty bad. I feel really sad when that happens."

- "I am feeling pretty disappointed. You are not staying in your seat like I asked, and being out of your seat disturbs the other students."

This may be enough to defuse the defensiveness and begin a genuine conversation about the student's behavior. Its success is more likely if the student actually cares about how you feel (most do, although many do not want to show it). If, however, the student answers by saying, "Who cares?" then smile and calmly use this response: "I just wanted to let you know how I feel." Then, still smiling, break eye contact, turn slowly, and walk away, having had the last word.

Another variation is to state how you feel about something the student is doing, followed by an invitation for the student to help you resolve the problem.

Examples:

- "Betty, I feel a little angry when you are whispering when I am trying to teach. Can you help me with that?" (Non-example: "Betty, you are making too much noise. You need to stop whispering when I am talking.")

- "Ethan, I get frustrated when you call out answers before other students have a chance to respond. Can you help me find a way to let you and others in the class know when you can answer?" (Non-example: "Ethan, if I've told you once I've told you a thousand times, raise your hand before calling out answers!")

- "Class, I am finding it difficult to teach when so many of you are getting out of your seats. What can we do to solve this problem?" (Non-example: "OK class, you don't seem to remember that you should be in your seats unless you have permission. If I don't see everyone in their seats in 30 seconds, you will all stay in for recess!")

Call the parents. In this day of cell phones and instant access, some teachers keep a listing of parent home and work numbers handy and are now having the student call his or her parents right there in the hallway. The student dials the number, the teacher takes the phone and explains that there has been a problem in the class, and then gives the phone back to the student to tell what happened. The teacher takes the phone back and asks the parent to follow up with the student at home tonight. The teacher then thanks the parent for his or her support, and the intervention concludes. Be sure to inform parents of this practice in your discipline disclosure handouts.

In rare situations a parent might object to being interrupted at work. Your response to this objection should be simple but direct: "I also object to being interrupted at my work. The purpose of my call is to find a way that, together, you and I can keep this from happening again. I would appreciate your help in helping Trey to understand this."

This intervention is helpful if parents are interested and involved. Sadly, that is not always the case, as you will quickly learn. Fortunately, you have the other structured tactics to use.

Remember, the "I Message" also works with parents:

Example:

• "Mr. Gerber, I feel bad that Todd has been having so many behavior problems this month. Is there anything that you could suggest that would help me to help him? Perhaps anything that previous teachers have done that seemed to work?" (Non-example: "Your son is way too disruptive in class. You need to straighten him out right away or he will be spending the rest of the year in the office!")

"Reality Therapy." With the goal of helping the student to assess his or her own behavior and subsequently take responsibility for it, William Glasser (1977) suggested the following sequence of steps in a process he called "reality therapy." This process begins by engaging the student in his or her own analysis of what happened and concludes with the student's own plan to resolve the problem. There are six steps to this procedure, which structure your private conference with the student:

1. Lead with empathy.

2. What did you do?

3. Did it help?

4. Make a plan.

5. Make a commitment to follow the plan.

6. Follow up.

1. LEAD WITH EMPATHY. If the student enters the conference visibly upset or shaken, start by acknowledging the feelings the student is experiencing. Indeed, because that emotional overlay will color everything that must follow, it is the elephant in the room that must be recognized before you can move on.

- "Looks like you are pretty upset."

- "I can see you're still pretty angry."

- "If that happened to me, I'd be feeling pretty bad, too."

- "Sounds like this hasn't been a good day for you."

2. WHAT DID YOU DO? "Mike, tell me what happened." Having heard Mike's perspective on the situation, you want him to articulate what actions he took or the role he played in it. These may be actions that instigated the situation, contributed to the situation, or came in response to the actions of others. The point is that he is responsible for what actions he took. "What did you do?"

is the key question. It is essential that the student own his responsibility by articulating what he did. It is likely that you will need to repeat this question several times until he can tell you what he did. Students have learned to blame others and create smoke screens to camouflage any responsibility they have. Your response to this ploy is the technique known as the broken record, repeating the question over and again until the student really answers it.

- "I understand, but what did *you* do?"

- "Yes, I realize that, but what did *you* do?"

- "OK, that much is clear, but what did *you* do?"

3. DID IT HELP? It is also important that the student recognizes and acknowledges that his behavior was inappropriate. Rather than telling him he was wrong, you want Mike to make his own judgment about his actions. This is part of being responsible. This step is very brief but critical to help the student accept responsibility. You accomplish this by asking only one question, such as:

- "Was this the right thing to do?"

- "Was this helpful to you?"

- "What was the effect on other students in the class?"

- "Was this helping our class to be a better place to learn?"

- "Were you breaking or following the rules [law]?"

4. MAKE A PLAN. This step is the most important—don't leave the conference without it. All too often we impose an action or consequence, thereby absolving the student of responsibility. Before Mike rejoins the class, we want him to have developed a plan for changing his behavior. It must be his own plan. This may be an entirely new experience for him.

It is too easy for us to jump in with solutions and ideas. We're experts in this area. But doing so is not really so helpful to the student. This may be fairly difficult for some. Students often lack the experience or insight to think of viable options on their own. It is so much easier to let you just tell them what to do. Give them time to think about it for a bit. Say you will check back in a little while to see how it's coming.

If after a reasonable time no ideas are forthcoming, Jim Fay (1995, p. 95) suggests that we simply ask if he would like you to recommend some ideas. By asking first, you are communicating that the ownership of this problem is still the student's.

- "Would you like to hear what others have tried?"

- "I have some ideas that might help. Would you like to hear them?"

- "I once had another student who had a similar problem to solve. Would you like to know what he did?"

Once you receive permission, share some possible ideas. Lead with "Some kids . . ." and avoid the more prescriptive "You need to . . . ."

- (damaged property) "In a similar situation, some people will go up to her and say they are sorry. Others might bring her a new one from home. Still others have tried offering to pay for it." Do any of those sound workable for you? Can you think of any others?"

- (classroom misbehavior) "Some kids say they are sorry and promise to make up their missed work at home. Some ask if they can change their seat in the room. Some suggest that they help clean up the classroom during recess. Have you thought of any others?"

He needs to select one of the alternatives you have discussed and tell you what he will now do to rectify the situation. If he can't seem to make a decision, leave him to think about it for a while, then check back. This again affirms where the responsibility lies. If there is still no progress, try a statement like this:

"I have some ideas on solving that. Most kids like their own ideas best. But if you don't have any ideas you think will work for you by 2:00, we will go with mine."

You may ask older students to write down their plan and sign it. His plan may not be the best plan, but unless it has major flaws, let him try it. If his plan doesn't work, he will simply have to develop another one.

"Sorry, you already tried that out and it didn't work. Now I need you to come up with a different plan."

5. MAKE A COMMITMENT. Finally, because you want Mike to try out his plan, get a commitment from him that he will. He does this by shaking hands with you, making a verbal commitment (promise) that he will do it, or writing down the plan and signing it. Once he has selected a plan of action and made a commitment to complete the plan, you want him to know that you trust he will actually complete it.

- "Good luck with your plan. Let me know how it went."

- "Feel free to eat in the cafeteria again when the mess is taken care of."

- "I'll check back with you tomorrow to see how your plan worked for you."

6. FOLLOW UP. Some time later in the day or during the next day, call Mike aside and ask how his plan is going. "Did you try your plan? How is it going?" If he has not started, ask when he will. Then have him see you when he does so you will know how it went. If his plan did not go well, you can help him make adjustments in it, model some new language to use, or simply have him develop a new plan. If it worked, congratulations are in order.

Some teachers (and principals) have found it helpful to structure these steps into a form that the student completes independently in advance of the conference. This provides an additional delay to cool the emotions and moves the student toward a more rational frame of mind. In the subsequent face-to-face conference, the completed form becomes the framework for the conversation.

"Logical Consequences." Not all misbehavior involves breaking a rule that has a posted consequence in the classroom discipline plan, and punishment is often not the most effective way to teach appropriate behavior. Sometimes you will need to confront a problem by devising a logical consequence. Rudolf Dreikurs (1972, p. 89) taught us that a consequence is logical (or natural) when it follows naturally from the behavior, not when it is arbitrarily imposed. These consequences make sense to the student and the class. If this connection is not clear, it will not be effective. There is a dual purpose here. Not only is a just consequence applied, but the student gains a learning experience. When the student must help devise a consequence (with some level of teacher assistance, depending on the age of the student), the process develops a stronger sense of responsibility. Building on the work of Dreikurs, Jane Nelsen (2006) tells us that effective logical consequences must be:

- Related to the problem

- Respectful to the student

- Reasonable, not excessive or overly punitive

- Revealed in advance

We need to use care that our logical consequences come across as helpful, not as punishments in disguise. We must focus on solutions, not ways to make students feel bad.

During a little quiet time in the evening or on the weekend, consider situations in which students are not meeting your academic or behavior expectations. What natural consequence would follow that behavior in the working world or in the marketplace? For what completely justifiable reason did you establish this expectation? The answers to these questions will help you to plan out some logical consequences that you can impose, and do so without anger because they are so inherently reasonable.

BEHAVIOR	LOGICAL CONSEQUENCE	ARBITRARY PUNISHMENT
Student turns in a sloppy paper	Student must rewrite the paper	Teacher refuses to accept it, student given 0 points
Student leaves textbook at home	Student must ask someone else to share	Teacher gives the student another textbook
Student enters class making too much noise	Student must leave class and re-enter quietly	Student is docked five academic points on today's grade
Student loses a borrowed paperback novel	Student works out a way to replace the novel	Teacher scolds the student and changes his desk
Two students get in a heated argument at recess	Students separated, given cooling-off time, each told to develop a plan of action	Students directed to each miss one week of recess

The application of a logical consequence may also take place in your private conference. In such a situation, the teacher confronts the student with the behavior, makes a judgment that the behavior is not acceptable, and explains the need for a solution (logical consequence). Set a deadline to begin and/or complete the consequence, and then make a note to remind yourself to follow up. As always, do all of this calmly and in a completely matter-of-fact, professional manner.

CHAPTER 6

Professionalism:

KEEPING IT ALL TOGETHER

● ● ●

Just as important as having a repertoire of strategies for managing student behavior is having strategies for "keeping it all together."
First among these is having a written behavior plan. This is a plan that keeps students, parents, and the principal informed about how you will typically respond to routine behavior issues. Because you have so many other options for handling behavior, this plan is your fallback position to be used when you need it. It is clear, concise, systematic, progressively severe, and includes a component for positive incentives.

The second strategy for keeping it all together is to teach and use routines. Routines are the structures that provide security for students and relief for teachers. They make expectations clear and provide the license for students to act with some independence without disrupting the class or distracting the teacher.

The third strategy is to stay alert and aware of what is going on in your class. Teachers who are not aware are teachers in trouble. It is when one student or a small group of students is allowed to occupy the teacher's attention that the rest of the class gets the signal that the coast is clear. Supervision is on hold. Expectations are not enforced. It's time to kick back and take a little break. It's much like diversionary tactics in the military. The lesson here: stay alert and stay with it.

The fourth strategy is to keep your cool. Part of being a professional is to remain calm in the face of challenges. You are in charge of your class and your students need you to stay calm and in control. Teachers who lose their temper lose the respect and confidence of their students. They also run the risk of saying or doing things that they will have difficulty defending in the future. Think of your classroom as a fishbowl and conduct yourself with the professional demeanor that you would want the world to see and respect.

Finally, now that you have all of these strategies at your command, how do you incorporate them into a class that is already well into the school year? To take a piecemeal approach is to defend and justify each one as it is rolled out, making the change process much more complicated. Change that occurs too frequently has the effect of destabilizing the class environment. When students begin to believe that their environment is not stable, the rate of misbehavior will increase. It is their way of trying to determine where the limits really are. To avoid this problem, present your new management practices as a new package for the operation of your classroom that will be followed for several weeks to come. Then follow it with consistency.

STRATEGY 20 ▶ Adopt a Formal Management Structure

Fairness is one of the most fundamental values in our country. We want predictability in our environment, and we want to know the rules before we are held accountable to follow them. Once the rules are disclosed, we expect that everyone else will be held to the same standard. "After all," we explain, "that would be only fair."

Most of our students come to us with that same value firmly embedded in them, just as most parents demand treatment they perceive as even-handed from the beginning of the year. So we develop formal structures that give students and parents the reassurance they need, as well as giving us a practical tool for managing a classroom in a fair manner. These structures describe expectations, negative consequences, positive incentives, and they provide some format for tracking student behavior. We publish our structure the first week of school and post it in the room as a reminder. These structures have

Formal Structures for Managing Behavior

- Clear expectations

- Progressive consequences

- Behavior tracking plan

- Positive incentives

- Open disclosure

become a basic component of nearly every classroom in the country because they are such effective tools of communication.

Typically, teachers carefully work out a formal plan of response when misbehavior occurs: a plan that contains clear expectations, a set of progressively severe consequences, incentives when your expectations are met, and open disclosure to build trust and predictability. As with any plan, revisions and adjustments will be needed as you learn from your experiences with each unique class. Many schools now require minimum components in each teacher's plan, so it will be important to find out if there are any such expectations in your school. Other teachers on the faculty who already have effective formal structures can be helpful as you develop or fine-tune a formal structure of your own.

A word of caution on the use of formal structures, however: in some classrooms they are applied much too rigorously. You must temper the procedures and expectations with your good judgment. Not every student comes to the class with the same capabilities. Not every third infraction requires a severe consequence in order to bring about change. While your formal structure will save you a lot of grief and time, you will still need to make exceptions to a lockstep response and exercise your own professional discretion in some situations. Extenuating circumstances do matter. This is why I have included so many other intervention strategies in Chapter 5. It is important that you be alert to the possibility of a special circumstance and gain the confidence to exercise judgment when special care is needed.

Clear expectations. We explored your expectations for student behavior in Strategy 8 and provided a number of examples. We mention it again in this section to underscore how important it is for you to be clear about how you want your students to behave *before* you use a management plan. The critical values of fairness, consistency, and open disclosure are all grounded in clear expectations. Remember the value of including a compliance rule as described in Strategy 8.

Progressive consequences. So what if Ken breaks a rule? Usually the most minimal intervention you provide will be enough to correct that behavior. If he breaks it a second time on the same day, we try something a little more assertive in order to get his attention. Yet again? It is now clear that Ken needs to know that 1) we are serious about this expectation, 2) that we still do not have his attention, and 3) that a more serious consequence will now be applied. (See the examples on page 119.)

FORMAL CONSEQUENCES. When formal consequences are needed, they should be applied in a progressive sequence of severity and/or coordinate with any school-wide plans that your school may have.

Examples of Progressive Consequences

1st	Warning
2nd	Miss 10 minutes of recess
3rd	Parents called, miss lunch recess
4th	Move to back of class, parent meeting to develop a new plan
5th	Office visit

1st	Verbal warning
2nd	Change seat
3rd	Written explanation of what happened and what he will now do
4th	Student calls parents
5th	Office referral

Behavior tracking plan. You will need a system to track the number of rule infractions individual students are making. This could be a huge imposition on you if you had not already put in place the prevention strategies described in Chapters 2, 3, and 4. Because you have, misbehavior should not be a common occurrence at this point. Having a tracking system gives you the information you need to administer your system of progressive consequences. Here is the important fringe benefit: using the tracking system can be, in itself, an intervention. When students see you silently making marks or giving tickets, they have their reminder. In this case, actions do speak louder than words.

Behavior-Tracking Plan Ideas

▲ One way to track student disruptions is to simply write the name of the student in a designated area on the board. Each time there is a repeat disruption, place a check mark next to the student's name. You don't need to say anything for the first few marks, just continue teaching. The consequences can then be applied later when you have time and without stopping you from teaching. The number of check marks corresponds to a progressively severe consequence.

▲ Some teachers will use a set of color-coded cards, one set for each student, placed in a pocket chart on the wall. Each color beneath the first means a progressively more severe consequence. When Andy breaks a rule, you instruct him to "pull a card." As you continue teaching without further disruption, Andy then gets out of his seat, walks over to the bulletin board where the pocket chart is posted, pulls the first card, and places it at the back of his set, revealing the next color in his set. The consequence that corresponds to that color of card applies later when you have time to talk to Andy without interrupting your lesson.

▲ Students can be given a ticket similar to a traffic ticket for rule infractions. You simply write his or her name on the stub (which you keep to track these infractions) and give the ticket to the student as a warning. No words are needed; the message has been sent.

Positive incentives. When the class meets your expectations, the students need some signal that they have been successful and that you are pleased with their behavior. Some individual students who have struggled with your expectations may need a little more recognition than others. Positive incentives provide you the tool to give that recognition. They also contribute to a positive classroom environment where success and cooperation is appreciated. Here are a few ideas for class-wide reinforcers:

- Use some favorite background music during independent work.

- If your district allows, give students 15 minutes of free time at the end of the day, or 30 minutes at the end of the week. You may consider allowing the class to leave for recess two minutes early.

- Randomly give out red tickets when you "catch" students behaving well. Have the students write their name on the back of the red ticket and drop it into a jar for a weekly drawing. At the close of Friday, have a drawing for extra school supplies, cheap trinkets, or a pass on one homework assignment.

- Drop a marble in a jar when the class is meeting your expectations. Even when students are quietly working in their seats, the sound of the marble hitting the jar will be an audible signal of your approval. When the jar is so full that you can no longer screw down the lid, the class has earned the promised incentive.

▲ Be sure that any incentives you choose do not contribute to our growing concern about childhood obesity. You can find ideas for healthy classroom incentives on the following Web sites:

http://specialed.about.com/cs/behaviordisorders/a/rewards.htm

http://www.eatsmartmovemorenc.com/EatSmartSchoolStds/Texts/rewards_incentives.pdf

Open disclosure. Expectations, consequences, and incentives should not be a secret. You can pretty much assume that your classroom is a fishbowl with 30 pairs of eyes seeing what is going on and interpreting what is seen by others (like their parents). Openly discuss your classroom management plan as the year begins and be very willing to talk about what it is and the reasons you have designed it as you have.

If you are a new teacher, I would advise starting with your mentor, an experienced teacher who can give you his or her insight and advice before you actually launch your plan. Then take a copy to your principal. Ask for his or her feedback and advice, indicating that you will be sending out copies to the parents and you would like administrative approval before you do. Once it is approved, post the plan in the room for students to see and for future reference. Include your expectations, consequences, and incentives, and discuss it thoroughly with the class. Take the time to actually teach your expected behaviors: modeling examples, eliciting non-examples, rehearsing each expected behavior, providing feedback, and practicing signals. (See Strategy 16.)

It's always a good idea to send home copies to the parents of your students. (Consider asking parents to sign a copy and send it back.) Be sure new students and their parents also receive a copy. Include a written invitation for parents to schedule time to meet with you if they have any questions or concerns about your plan. Have extra copies of your plan available for parent-teacher conferences, should questions arise.

STRATEGY 21 ▸ Teach and Use Routines

Imagine that every time people went to the library they had to learn a new set of procedures for finding and checking out books. It would be bedlam. Classrooms are similar. When students know the routine, they are more likely to behave in the way you expect.

Routines save teachers time, give students security, increase the odds of having a successful lesson, and improve classroom efficiency. When students know what to do and how to do it, the likelihood that they will misbehave drops markedly. Because students are taking care of routine business on their own, teachers are free to focus on instruction.

I have worked with a number of teachers who had to break from their lesson in order to give special directions for sharpening a pencil or passing out a worksheet. I have watched a high school science teacher regularly take more than ten minutes to take roll, get homework assignments turned in, and sign the various notes and excuses that students brought to class. Over the course of a year in a 50-minute class period, that is 36 days of lost instruction! I have seen second grade students take ten minutes to simply pick up a worksheet and return to their desks, talking and jostling each other all the way.

Do yourself a favor and teach specific procedures for handling those routine tasks. It will save you time and aggravation, build confidence and independence in your students, reduce incidents of misbehavior, and improve learning

Five Essential Starter Routines

- Sharpening pencils

- Taking roll

- Distributing and collecting materials

- Restrooms and drinks

- Early completers

in your class. Talk to your mentors, department chairs, or senior teachers to find out what routines they use. There are hundreds. Listed in this strategy are a few to get you started.

Sharpening pencils. The pencil breaks. Is it now OK to get up and wander around the room? Is this the perfect chance to whisper to friends or pass a note? Must we all now wait while the noisy sharpener grinds and grinds? If the student is denied permission to sharpen his pencil, does this mean students can now kick back and enjoy being excused from the assigned work? Does pencil breaking ever become contagious in the room?

Try this routine. Sharpen a dozen brand new pencils and place them in a small plastic box. When a pencil point breaks, the student raises his or her hand, and you swap out the pencil, noting the student's name. At the end of the class, the student swaps back. Each morning you will want to be sure that you have a full supply of sharpened pencils. No wandering around, no disruptive grinding noise, no incentives to break a pencil, no missed work.

Another pencil routine is to keep a box of golf pencils on hand. Again, students who need a pencil can borrow one of the teacher's. It's not as nice, but if that is a problem for the student, he or she might prefer to bring his or her own spare pencil.

Taking roll. Never take roll by calling out every student's name. It takes far too much time and creates an activity void that will be quickly filled with misbehavior. Try this instead: assign students to their desks and make a seating chart. Some teachers place a small picture of the student on the seating chart along with the name. While they are working independently on their self-starter (see Strategy 3), simply look around the class to see who is missing and mark the roll. Not only does this accomplish the task and keep the students busy, it provides a substitute teacher with a practical way to keep order.

Another option is to keep a card or a student folder by the door to the classroom. (Middle school teachers will need to divide these by class period.) Instruct students to pick up their card or folder as they enter the room. Cards or folders left by the door when the bell rings indicate the students who are absent or tardy. The teacher marks the roll as students complete their self-starter activity. The use of a folder also provides a means of distributing papers to students and collecting papers at the end of class.

Distributing and collecting materials. Probably the least efficient practice I have seen is when a teacher walks around the room handing each student a piece of paper. It is a prime example of a practice that creates an engagement void that invites students to misbehave. There are several options to solve this. Get the students involved, have them help. Give stacks of papers to the first person in each row and have them pass them back. Give the entire stack of handouts to one student and have him or her distribute them to the rows or tables. Have students pass their papers to the person in front or to the right. Place a basket on a counter and have the students place completed work in the basket at the end of class or just before recess. Assign one person from each table to come forward to pick up or deliver materials on behalf of their table.

Restrooms and drinks. A stream of students moving in and out of class for a drink or to use the restroom is not only disruptive to the rest of the class, it also creates opportunities for misbehavior. Certainly students have a chance to get a drink of water during a class change or at recess, and going without water for an hour or two is unlikely to make anyone sick. While using the restroom to prevent an embarrassing accident is both reasonable and a basic entitlement, frequent use of the restroom for emergencies without a medical note is out of line.

Many middle schools are now having students take a hall pass with them. It is big, bright, and obvious. Only one hall pass is allocated per class, with the room number written on it. Only one student per class is allowed in the hall at a time. The student must still raise his or her hand to get permission to use the hall pass. This gives you the opportunity to continue with your lesson with a minimum of disruption and reduces their incentive to leave class. You should document chronic use of the hall pass by a student and involve parents to either help resolve the problem or shed light on a special physical condition that requires a special accommodation.

Early completers. Some of the most challenging behaviors we encounter come from our brightest students. Those who complete their work early and then have nothing to do often fill in the time by taking others off task. Because you are monitoring the work and behavior of the rest of the class, you do not always have time to give this group a special lesson followed by a special assignment. Giving early completers a routine to follow when they complete their work early takes the pressure off as it enriches the lesson for them. Try some of these options:

- Give them a long-term assignment (report, poster, presentation to prepare, etc.) that is related to the curriculum and takes it to a deeper and more complex level. This is the kind of work they can begin on their own and continue working on when they complete their assignments early.

- Keep a box of reading cards, a trivia book, or a book of strange facts handy. When their work is completed, these students can quietly select one, return to their desk, and read it independently.

Classroom Management • 24 Strategies Every Teacher Needs to Know

- Have extra-credit assignments related to the lesson on hand.

- Write an open-ended topic on the board each day. When waiting for the rest of the class to complete its work, students can write a one-page response to the topic in their journal.

- Have students keep a novel from the library in their desk at all times. If they complete their work early and have nothing else to do, they can take out their book and read.

- Use a computer center in the class for students to work on a computer-assisted assignment or do some Internet-based research.

A caveat: Periodically check to be sure that work is both complete and accurate. Only then will they be considered an "early completer." Give others their paper back, with the directive to complete the assignment properly.

STRATEGY 22 ▶ Keep Up

You need to know what's happening in your class. You need to keep up. In the words of Jacob Kounin (1970, p. 81), we need to "have eyes behind our heads." Kounin was the first to use the term "withitness" to describe the teacher who remains "with it," or aware of what is happening in all parts of the classroom at all times. When you notice that a student is behaving inappropriately, you intervene immediately and accurately before that behavior accelerates into a disruption that requires a more intrusive intervention. This has a ripple effect on the entire class. An intervention is a

Essential Components to Keep Up

- Scan the class.

- Buffer the interruptions.

- Avoid procedures that encourage distractions.

- Intervene in a timely, accurate fashion.

signal to students that you are aware of what they are doing and are serious about your expectations. This is particularly important at the beginning of the year and applies across all age levels. In his meta-analysis, Marzano (2003) found that the disruptions in the classrooms of teachers who were "with it" were no less that 42 percentile points lower than in the classrooms of teachers who were not.

REFLECTION QUESTION

Do I really know what's going on in my classroom?

To keep up with what is going on in your class, you start by frequently scanning the room. You can scan as you walk around, deliver a lecture, conduct a discussion, work with a small group, or even talk to an individual student. The strategy of proximity control is also a strategy for keeping up with your class. (See Strategy 4.) You cannot stay "with it" if your attention is too narrowly focused on a single student or small group, so you carefully manage interruptions in your class. You review your classroom procedures to be sure that they do not encourage distractions. Finally, you intervene in a timely manner, accurately identifying the students who are misbehaving. (See the interventions listed in Strategy 17.)

Scan the class. It is sad to watch a teacher deliver a carefully crafted lesson completely unaware that a small group of students in the back of the class is carrying on their own private conversation. You need to know what your students are doing at all times. This is done with a quick scan of the room.

A scan means taking a quick look around the class to see who is and who is not on task. It means listening for unusual sounds. When you scan, quickly look at every face; it is the eyes that tell you where their attention lies. Scanning is a constant activity for effective teachers. What you don't know is happening *can* hurt you.

A dynamic proximity helps. When you are moving throughout the room, your scanning is more effective because your perspective is also changing. You can see more faces; more hidden corners are brought into the light, and you can detect covert side conversations. You know what is happening in your class. Knowing that empowers you to act when an intervention is necessary. It empowers to correct a situation before it gets out of hand. It communicates to the students that they are not invisible, and they can be held accountable. Make it your business to know what is happening in your class. (See Strategy 4.)

Buffer the interruptions. An all too common mistake for new teachers is to allow themselves to become so focused on an individual that they temporarily lose their connection with the rest of the class. It often is precisely during that focused interruption that problems begin to pop up. You need to be aware of this possibility and take steps to prevent it from undermining classroom behavior.

This is certainly an easy mistake to make. A student asks a good question during quiet seatwork, and we are excited to take the time to explore the answer. A project or experiment requires teacher help before a small group can move on. A special-needs student requires a separate explanation for an alternative assignment. A girl walks in during a lesson with a message from the office asking for an immediate reply. All of these situations create an interruption in your supervision. That interruption is a point of risk for classroom management.

However, even during an interruption you can maintain your awareness. You can pause in your conversation to stand up and scan the class. You can "interrupt the interrupter" to use social cues and nonverbal interventions by simply saying, "Excuse me a minute." You can ask a student or office aide to wait for a minute until you can take the question or read the note. You can take care to never have your back to the center of the class during independent seatwork. You can stand up during a change of small groups to monitor the transition.

Avoid procedures that encourage distractions. Some classroom procedures actually encourage distractions. Teachers who sit at their desk and have students come to that desk with questions may be creating a human picket fence between the teacher and the class. Teachers who have their back to the class while they are teaching a small group place themselves at a great disadvantage. Teachers who personally pass out and collect papers and materials create a window of opportunity for misbehavior. Students who are tardy can be directed to see you during recess instead of interrupting class to update your roll book. Investigations of student complaints can wait until a more convenient time, instead of taking the teacher's attention away from supervising the class. Teachers who are exclusively tied to the whiteboard or to an overhead projector unintentionally grant a "free parking" pass to students in the back half of the class. Teachers who sit at their desk correcting papers while students are supposed to be quietly doing seatwork are inviting misbehavior.

Intervene in a timely, accurate fashion. When you notice a student misbehaving, you need to quickly use one of the intervention methods described in Strategy 17. That is the purpose of scanning: to notice with "eyes in the back of your head" and intervene. Be sure that your intervention correctly identifies the student(s) involved. To intervene with the wrong student not only embarrasses and angers the student singled out, but it also signals the class that you don't really know what is going on in your own room.

A minor intervention is usually all that is needed to have a major effect. The effect is not only on the student misbehaving, but on the entire class. The fact that the class noticed that you intervened has another kind of ripple effect on everyone, and the class's engagement rate rises, even though you only delivered this minor intervention to one student.

When you notice through your scanning that the class is working well, this is also time to use the social cue described in Strategy 1. In this context, the social cue can have a similar ripple effect that helps maintain appropriate behavior. Again, you need to notice, and you notice through scanning.

STRATEGY 23 ▶ Keep Your Cool

Teaching is a very personal activity. It matters to us deeply, and student defiance tends to hurt us at that deep personal level. We react. When that reaction surfaces as screaming, throwing things, upsetting furniture, or stomping out of the class, we do more harm than good. In fact, we even end up damaging ourselves. To be calm is to project strength. To lose control is to project weakness. When we model tantrums, we invite students to tantrum. When we "lose it," we legitimize students who "lose it." When we scream at our class, we make screaming an acceptable student response to an affront. Worse yet, when we lose our cool, we risk damaging a child.

Rick Wormeli (2003) strongly advises that we do not allow our anger to cause us to lash back at our students. "Avoid all insults and put-downs. This is a hurtful response and it doesn't teach the student anything except that it's acceptable to hurl insults in the adult world. It makes you look weak, too, for adults are supposed to be more mature than that."

We need to model the behavior we want to see in our students. We need to remain calm, composed, and rational. We are the adults, and it is our responsibility to model adult behavior. When challenges arise and the stress levels climb, we smile because we are in control of the situation. Our movements are slow and deliberate, we speak in a calm and controlled voice, we project confidence. We act in a way that preserves and develops positive relationships, not threatens them.

If you find that this is a challenge for you, here are a few strategies that might help:

Smile, move slowly, get close, use a soft voice. Take a deep breath. Begin with a smile. Move slowly toward the student(s). Get to the student's eye level. Use a soft voice. If these sound tough for you, practice them at home first.

You have options. Remind yourself that this is a teaching moment, and you have a full bag of tricks with a number of strategies to deal with it. (See Chapter 5.)

"Tell me what happened." If you pull a student aside, start by asking the student to describe what happened. (There is always another side to the story.) This will give you time to cool off and start the conversation by looking at facts. When we move into the realm of facts and figures, the emotional pressures of the moment begin to wane.

Seat away. When the pressure is building, delay your response. The use of "seat away," scheduling an appointment during recess or a prep period, or even "Wait for me in the hall" are all strategies that give you distance from your emotional reaction and time to cool down. The following lines are designed to help you disengage: "We need to talk about this, but I can't right now. I need to better understand your point of view. We'll have to continue this later."

Humor. If you can find something funny about the situation or an appropriate quip, use it. Humor has a magical quality that can take the edge off a confrontation or relieve some of the anger.

"Write it down." Buy yourself time and distance by having the student(s) in conflict write down their story and how they felt about what happened. Later, after the heat of the moment, you can meet with the students to review what they wrote. Not only will you be in a calmer state, but so will they.

Avoid a public confrontation. Move to a quiet place and speak to the student in private. It will ease some of the pressure for both you and the student.

Tape recorder. If allowed, leave a tape recorder running at a particularly difficult time and simply listen to yourself. Play it at home later (in private). It may give you some valuable insight about how you are being perceived. It might also give you some insight into yourself to help you adjust your own practices.

Take a deep breath. Use the old tried-and-true, time-honored tactics: count to ten, take five deep breaths, step into a restroom or closet, or think of your favorite place. (In a rage emergency, try stepping into the hall, putting a pillow in front of your mouth, and screaming to your heart's content. Then return to your room fully composed, smiling, and in control of the situation.)

STRATEGY 24 ▶ Getting Started . . . Again!

Explaining your management plan to your class is an essential step. Students need to know the rules before they can comply with them. They need to know your signals and the procedures they will be expected to follow. They also need to know that logic underlies your management plan to understand that it is necessary for the orderly operation of the class, not simply to assert the authority of the teacher.

The easiest time to teach your management plan is during the first week of school. But sometimes we need to make major adjustments in our plan in the course of the year. If the changes are major, you have a tactical decision to make. You can roll out those changes piecemeal, which is not a bad decision if you have only a few minor adjustments to make. But if you are planning to launch a number of major changes, you can develop a plan carefully designed to maximize the impact of those changes.

Here's the temptation: we happen on a new idea and roll it out immediately. Then we come across another great idea and try it out as well. After three or four of these new ideas come at them every few days, your students will not be sure what they are doing or what is expected of them. They lose confidence in their ability to meet the teacher's expectations, and they lose confidence in the teacher's ability to direct and control the class with consistency. Unpredictability leads to misbehavior as students seek to operationally define the limits within which they must work. This can result in a perplexing conundrum: our attempts to improve the behavior of our students actually bring about a deterioration of classroom behavior!

An effective management plan is comprehensive, with all of the pieces disclosed in advance. It is fair and, because it is consistently applied to all students, it has integrity. It is reliable because it will be applied this week, next week, and the week after that. "In fact, this will be our plan until we have another class meeting and I announce any changes in the plan to all of you, at the same time, before those changes take place." To present it and then teach it to the class is to better assure its effectiveness.

Because we now have a new management plan, our tactical move is to roll it out all at once. Here's how you can do it:

When. Plan to launch your new plan at a logical break in the routine (e.g., following a holiday, the first day of a new term, after a long weekend).

Materials ready. Have your rules and procedures printed on posters, perhaps with a handout ready to be sent home to parents, explaining your new plan.

Prep the setting. Make the room look different to underscore your message that this class will be somehow different (e.g., dimmed lights, soft background music, new bulletin board colors, etc.).

Essential Steps to Getting Started . . . Again!

- Decide when to launch your new plan.

- Have any materials ready.

- Prep the setting.

- Alert students to the change before they enter the classroom.

- Explain the plan.

- Teach the plan.

- Use social cues.

- Stay with it.

Before they enter. Meet your class outside the room. Explain that there will now be some changes in our class and they are to walk in quietly and take their seats so you can explain those changes.

Explain the plan. Once they are seated, signal for their attention, then slowly and carefully explain the changes you have made. Allow time for questions.

Teach the plan. For new procedures and/or new classroom rules, take the time to explicitly teach them using a prompt, model, and practice format. (See Strategy 8.)

Use social cues. Use social cues to remind students of the new expectations, and verbal reinforcement when they meet these new expectations.

Stay with it. Stay with it for at least three weeks. It will take that long for your changes to become routines. Your adjustments are more likely to get the results you are looking for if they are few in number, carefully explained in advance, and understood because they're tied logically into the rest of the plan.

CHAPTER 7

Teaching Is a Team Sport:
GETTING HELP WHEN HELP IS NEEDED

• • •

If you are in your first years of teaching and finding it stressful and emotionally exhausting, you are in good company. Most of us have been there. In fact, I don't know a single teacher who'd like to repeat the early years. The good news is this: you don't need to endure it alone. Help is available for those who ask.

Where to Turn

INFORMAL CONVERSATIONS. Simply having someone to talk to can make a difference. Strike up a casual relationship with another teacher on your grade level, in your department, or just in the next room. When you have developed a level of trust, informal conversations with a colleague have a valuable therapeutic effect and help us to process stressful incidents or organize our thoughts about persistent problems.

TALK TO YOUR PRINCIPAL. He or she is the person who has the most information about what help is available in your schools and how to get it. Remember that in most cases this person has also been a teacher, and he or she also faced difficulties in that first year. In some schools the principal also serves in the role of mentor for new teachers. It is always in the best interest of the principal and the school to help a new teacher become successful.

TALK TO YOUR MENTOR. More and more schools and school districts are developing teacher mentor programs. A mentor is a teacher assigned to answer questions and familiarize the new teacher with school procedures and resources. Depending on the school, a mentor may also be someone who can observe in your class, make suggestions, and make arrangements for you to observe in another class to fine-tune the techniques of effective classroom management. The very existence of mentor teachers is the evidence that our profession now recognizes how critical those first few years of teaching can be.

TALK TO A SPECIALIST. Virtually every school in the country has access to a specialist. This could be a counselor, a resource teacher, a school psychologist, a social worker, or people who are trained in several other specialty fields of support. These specialists will have helpful suggestions for your most challenging students. They may also have suggestions drawn from what has worked in past years with those students in other teachers' classes. Some are assigned to the school full-time while others may be itinerant in the district. Check with your school office for available resources and how to access them.

Helpful Resources

There are some very fine resources in the field with other strategies for managing student behavior. Among them I would recommend:

Cooperative Learning by Spencer Kagan (Kagan Publishing, 1994)

The First Days of School: How to be an Effective Teacher by Harry Wong & Rosemary Wong (Harry K. Wong Publications, Inc., 2001)

Helping Teachers Engage Students: Action Tools for Administrators by A. Brinkman, G. Forlini, & E. Williams (Eye on Education, 2009)

Teaching With Love and Logic by Jim Fay & David Funk (The Love and Logic Press, 1995)

The Tough Kid Book: Practical Classroom Management Strategies by Ginger Rhode, William R. Jenson, & H. Kenton Reavis (Sopris West, 1994)

References

Breaux, A. & Wong, H. (2003). *New Teacher Induction: How to Train, Support, and Retain New Teachers*. Mountain View, CA: Harry K. Wong Publications, Inc.

Breaux, E. (2005). *Classroom Management Simplified*. Larchmont, NY: Eye on Education.

Brinkman, A. & Williams, E. (2005). *Student Habits for On-task Behavior*. Unpublished manuscript.

Brinkman, A., Forlini, G., & Williams, E. J. (2009). *Help Teachers Engage Students: Action Tools for Administrators*. Larchmont, NY: Eye on Education.

Cohen, L., Manion, L., & Morrison, K. (2004). *A Guide to Teaching Practice*. New York: Routledge.

Curwin, R. L. & Mendler, A. N. *Discipline With Dignity*. (1989). Alexandria, VA: Association for Supervision & Curriculum Development.

Dreikurs, R., Cassel, P., & Kehoe, D. (1972). *Discipline Without Tears*. New York: Hawthorn Books.

Dreikurs, R., Cassel, P., & Fergusen, E. (2004). *Discipline Without Tears: How to Reduce Conflict and Establish Cooperation in the Classroom*. Revised Edition. Hoboken, NJ: John Wiley & Sons.

Fadel, C. & Lemke, C. *Multimodal Learning Through Media: What the Research Says*, p. 46, 2008. http://www.cisco.com/web/strategy/docs/education/ Multimodal-Learning-Through-Media.pdf. Retrieved February 21, 2009.

Fay, J. & Funk, D. (1995). *Teaching With Love and Logic*. Golden, CO: The Love and Logic Press, Inc.

Fortin, C. *Management: The Elements. Four Steps to a Seamless Lesson*. April 27, 2008. http://classroom-management-tips.suite101.com/article.cfm/elements_of_ great_ class_management. Retrieved January 13, 2009.

Glasser, W. *The Quality School*. (1998). New York: Harper Collins Publishers, Inc.

Glasser, W. *Schools Without Failure*. (1977). New York: Harper and Row.

Gordon, T. (1974) *T.E.T.: Teacher Effectiveness Training*. New York: Random House.

Gudmundsen, A., Williams, E., & Lybbert, R. (1996). *You Can Control Your Class*. Novato, CA: Academic Therapy Publications.

Hunter, R., & Hunter, M. (2004). *Madeline Hunter's Mastery Teaching: Increasing Instructional Effectiveness in Elementary and Secondary Schools*. New York: Corwin Press.

Jones, F. *Tools for Teaching*. (2000). Santa Cruz, CA: Fredric H. Jones & Associates, Inc.

Jones, F., Jones, P., Jones, J., & Jones, B. (Illustrator). *Tools for Teaching: Discipline, Instruction, Motivation*. (2007). Mountain View, CA: Harry K. Wong Publications, Inc.

Kagan, S. (1994). *Cooperative Learning*. San Clemente, CA: Kagan Publishing.

Kounin, J. (1970). *Discipline and Group Management in Classrooms*. New York: Holt, Rinehart, and Winston.

Marzano, R. (2003). *Classroom Management That Works: Research Based Strategies for Every Teacher*. Alexandria, VA: Association for Supervision & Curriculum Development.

Nelson, J. *Positive Discipline*. (2006). New York: Random House.

Reynolds, L. L. *Multimodal Learning Through Media: What the Research Says*, p. 46, 2008. http://www.ehow.com/how_2181132_college-as-high-school-student.html. Retrieved December 23, 2008.

Rhode, G., Jenson, W., & Reavis, H. K. (1994). *The Tough Kid Book: Practical Classroom Management Strategies*. Frederick, CO: Sopris West.

Rowe, M. B. *"Wait Time: Slowing Down May Be a Way of Speeding Up."* American Educator 11 (Spring 1987): 38-43, 47. EJ 351 827.

Rutherford, P. (2002). *Why Didn't I Learn This in College?* Alexandria, VA: Just ASK Publications.

Schmitt, B. D. (1999). *Your Child's Health*. New York: Bantam Books.

Thaindian News. *Stressful Modern Life Has Reduced Attention Span to Just Five Minutes*. November 26, 2008. http://www.thaindian.com/newsportal/india-news/stressful-modern-life-has-reduced-attention-span-to-just-five-minutes_100123702.html. Retrieved January 13, 2009.

Wong, H. K. & Wong, R T. (2001). *The First Days of School: How to Be an Effective Teacher*. Mountain View, CA: Harry K. Wong Publications, Inc.

Wormeli, R. (2003). *Day One and Beyond*. Portland, ME: Stenhouse Publishers.

Seating Arrangement Ideas

Some younger grades have carpets that are used to bring the entire class close to the teacher for whole-class instruction while the teacher sits on a chair. Students alternately move from the carpet, back to their desks, and then again to the carpet as a strategy to accommodate their shorter attention span.

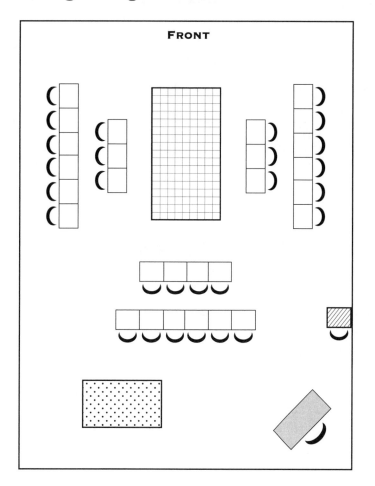

Another lower grade format is to use tables instead of desks, with four to six students at each table.

Students use tote trays to keep their books and papers in a separate area.

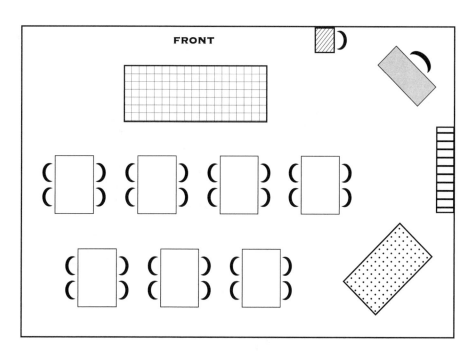

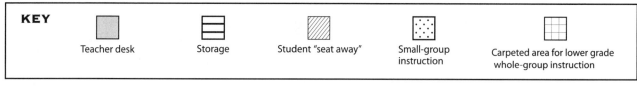

KEY

| Teacher desk | Storage | Student "seat away" | Small-group instruction | Carpeted area for lower grade whole-group instruction |

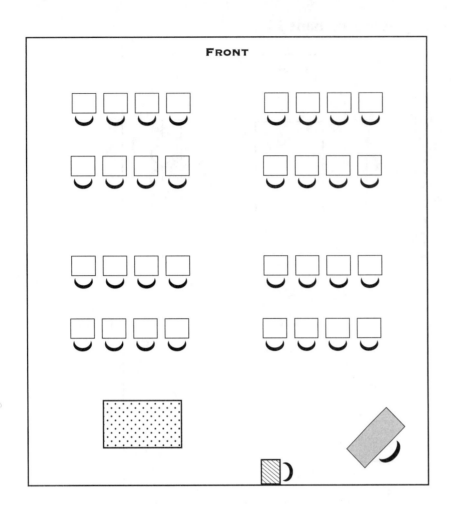

Teachers who prefer a more traditional format can still create a few broader aisles so that they can move quickly and easily around the room.

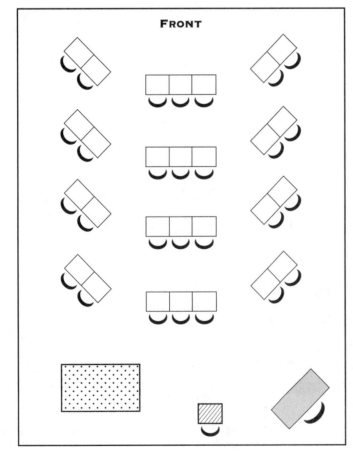

Clustering desks in groups of two or three predisposes the students to participate in teacher-directed pair-share and triad responses during the lesson.

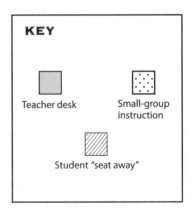

KEY

Teacher desk

Small-group instruction

Student "seat away"

Teachers who use small groups to increase student participation and engagement often arrange their room to be naturally conducive to these conversations. Students can see the front of the room by looking to the side, but can quickly and simultaneously respond to teacher questions with their peers.

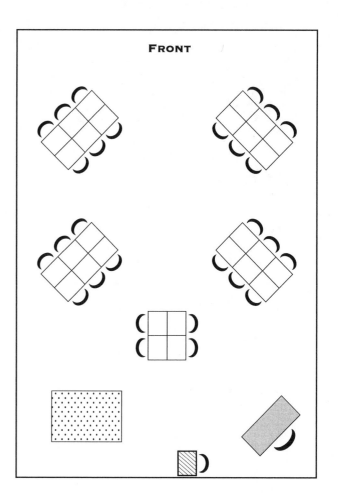

Clustered desks, commonly referred to as "tables," are particularly useful for small-group projects, reports, research, and differentiated assignments. Note how the teacher can easily move around the room to monitor these small-group discussions.

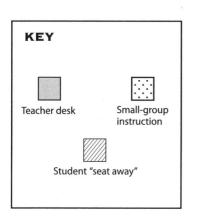

KEY

Teacher desk

Small-group instruction

Student "seat away"

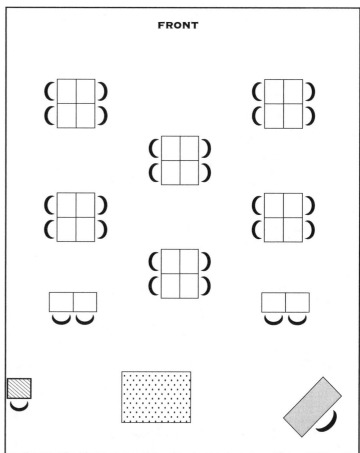

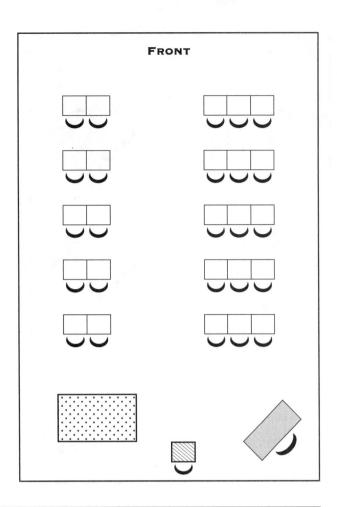

FRONT

Plenty of center space in this arrangement gives the teacher fluid access throughout the room and provides a convenient location for an overhead projector, multimedia projector, or document camera.

If space allows, an arrangement in which each half of the room has a single row of desks facing each other (not shown) allows the teacher to present from the center and every student to have a front row seat. It is also particularly useful when engaging in class-wide debates, legislative processes, or Socratic teaching approaches.

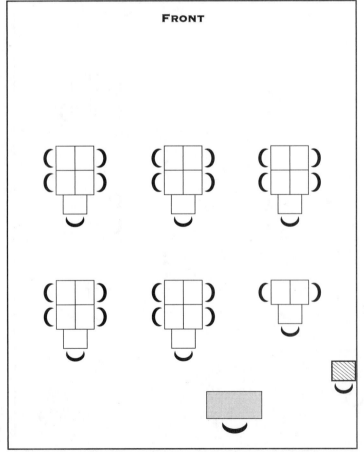

FRONT

Some teachers need space for large groups, particularly when using specialized equipment, laying out diagrams and maps, or performing dramatic works and role plays. Desks are still arranged to give the teacher easy access throughout the room.

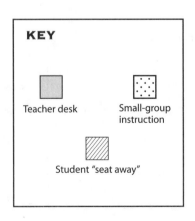

KEY

Teacher desk

Small-group instruction

Student "seat away"